OUT

OF THE

Shadows

AUDREY YAGALLA

A MEMOIR

ISBN (Print): 978-1-09837-140-1
ISBN (eBook): 978-1-09837-141-8

Table of Contents

Disclaimer

Some names have intentionally been changed or left out completely. The events within this memoir are recollections and recountings of events throughout my lifetime thus far. It is not my intent to cause ill will nor cause harm to anyone but rather to take readers on my personal journey towards wholeness. All healing modalities I have used served a purpose on my path to greater understanding and moving past the events set forth within this book. In writing my journey of healing, I wish for others to use their own personal compasses and discernment as they gain greater peace and understanding.

Dedication

This book is dedicated to my children and their children's children and all of humanity's generations to follow. To my children, I love you each to the end of the Universe and back. Within the revealing of these truths there is a complete letting go of all ancestral bindings through all points and times that have held us bound and gagged in oppression. It is in writing this memoir that our lives are set free of burdens and shadows that have lingered for far too long throughout our lives. May Divine Feminine rise fully and sit on Her rightful throne next to Divine Masculine.

What I have written upon these pages are my truths and expressions of my path through abuse by a cleric and to healing. Take what you will and leave the rest. It is my intention that this book offer you inspiration and hope towards a greater vision of what you are able to achieve within this lifetime for yourself and for your descendants. I offer this book to the ones who live within the shadows of their past. It is time to come out from hiding and rise like the light that you are destined to be. I offer you strength as you read and may anything that triggers you be easily and gracefully released fully for you to stand in your sovereignty.

I would like to take this opportunity to thank Dusk Weaver, the editor of this memoir, who was able to take more than nine years of musings and writings and help create a coherent book. I also want to thank my family members who have been there through the thick and thin of it all. I love you all and am grateful for your presence. I would also like to thank Mary Holden and Lisa B. for their wise editorial input in finalizing this book. I am grateful for your input, support, and encouragement.

To my teachers, Lorraine O., Carl K., Jami Hearn, Fred Salzman, Angell Deer, and countless others: thank you for your inspiration, knowledge and standing in your vision of missions and truths. It is with your guidance that I have the tools needed to grow into the being I am destined to become.

To Colbe Barrett, Soul Sloth Astrology, who explained my chart to me in such a brilliant way that I now own my unique way out-of-the-box thinking and embrace my unique role on this rotating sphere we call Earth.

To everyone I have encountered in this lifetime, you've each been a part of this journey, knowingly or unknowingly, as we each provide lessons and insights to each other along the way whether by way of example or mirror; thank you.

I would be remiss if I did not thank the people who have taught me about life, love, pain, sorrow, joy, and everything in between; you know who you are. And this is those who rejected me when I reached out when I felt that I needed support the most; your rejection was a catalyst to my continued healing and to my further understanding of humanity in all of it's humaneness.

To those who read and provided input into the draft of this book (Michelle, Stephanie, Brenda, Mary Jean, Ruth), thank you for your bravery, honest insight and guidance.

To my friends, Patti M., Wendy Y., Bill O'N, Debra W., Sarah J., Denika S., Holly P., Chris M., David who have seen me at my worst and still decided to stay, I am in gratitude to each of you and feel blessed to call you friend as we walk this journey.

Thank you to those who participated in the Pennsylvania grand jury whose voice was heard and whose voices continues to stir changes within the governmental systems. To those who continue to fight against the injustices that have plagued humanity, I commend you for your steadfastness in creating the changes. Thank you for speaking your truth. Thank you for standing up in solidarity creating the changes you wish to see in the world.

Allow Me to Introduce Myself

My given name is Audrey Yagalla, and I live in Pennsylvania, USA, the state in which my story begins. I was born the youngest of seven surviving children into a second-generation Polish immigrant working-class family but one with royal bloodlines. In addition to my earthly genetic background, I also know that I am one of many beings who volunteered to come here and help transform this planet's consciousness, to herald a new era of joyfulness and love with Mother Gaia.

The life journey I will share with you has often been grueling, and I have at times cried out for it to end, and yet I persisted and pushed forward. My roles on this planet are as a healer, helper, guide, and keeper of souls for those who have been looking for answers. I am a divine child of light, but I have known pain, great hardship, and brokenness. Mine has not been a path for the weak of heart, and there were often times when I thought my heart would break into a million pieces. But it did not, and I continue to rise. I rise knowing deep inside that I have a purpose, a purpose all mine and mine alone, just as you, too, have a purpose that is yours and yours alone.

Although my purpose is now so clear to me, and I shall share the specifics of it in these pages, a great deal of development was necessary before I could recognize it. Some of this development came in the form of highly supportive places and entities in my youth. For example, as a young child, I loved the solitude of walking in the woods and crossing streams to reach a special place in the forest. That forest was often my refuge, both in times of gentle growth as well as times of great stress. The earth angels and faeries there sat beside me as I sought a place to fit into the world.

There was also much other development – of a decidedly troubling nature – required in my life before I would even glimpse my purpose, and perhaps I can best describe this process overall as lessons gleaned from the school of hard knocks. I had few friends as a young child, and there was much loss in my childhood involving people that I loved. But then, capping those losses, my life took a horrifying traumatic dive that indelibly stamped not just my childhood but also the whole of my life, as well as the lives of so many others in my orbit. This plunge into horrifying trauma dominates the early chapters of this book, but it is ultimately *not* the defining theme of my life. Far from it, I am glad to say.

Studies of the human mind continue to show that the brain is one amazing computer, able to store memories, emotions, and experiences all neatly tucked away for later recall. In confront-ing extreme trauma, the brain is capable of compartmentalizing memories to an even greater degree, and it seems that the psyche under such duress sometimes fragments as a protective measure, whether the stress stems from an accident or an argument, from some great shock or a sellout of one's soul, no matter whether that stress is physical, emotional, or spiritual in nature. And some-times the psyche or soul recuperates, sometimes it does not.

There are healing methods that I have used throughout the years to mend from the traumatic events that beset me as a young-ster, and one modality in particular named Neuro-Linguistic Programming (aka NLP) provided me with significant healing. I shall describe this method in some detail after sharing my account of having come to need its benefits so desperately.

Throughout this book there is reference to a person named Father Skotek/Skotek, also known as Father Sko, Sko. To clarify, using the full name or nickname tended to be a trigger as I wrote and read the combination. It is not uncommon for re-traumati-zation to occur when seeing a title in front of the name for those who have been abused.

Within these pages, I will use the terms God, Universe, Universal Life Force, Creator of All That Is, and the One, all with the same reference to unlimited love, unlimited compassion, unlimited energy, and unlimited abundance of health, grace, and blessings. This is my higher power, one that we all have, and one from which no one is ever actually disconnected. That may not immediately resonate with some readers, but the reality is that we are all connected to something far greater than ourselves. And, we are connected to one another, so that if I were to deem some other person bad or negative, then I would effectively deem myself as such, too, because we are all connected to Christ Consciousness, or as it is also called, light consciousness. Each of us is his or her own universe. Each, one's own healer. Each, one's own spiritual counsel. Each, one's own master. When one begins to realize this, one no longer needs any intermediary connection to the higher powers of the Creator. It is inside us. It is through us. It is around us. It is us.

Furthermore, the incredibly supportive galactic beings known as Pleiadians have been with us for a very long time on this planet, carrying forth messages, codes, and activations that are needed to initiate a utopian matrix of harmony, love, and peace.

So what does all of this intriguing material have to do with my life story? It is directly related to the crushing darkness that engulfed my being and tried to quash my very soul, but a darkness that I have largely overcome. This, then, is my honest account of having fallen and arisen too many times to quit now.

I should like to conclude this introduction by sharing a message that I channeled from the beneficent Pleiadians while drawing up this account:

> So little in nature can be accurately expressed in terms of black and white. Most everything contains a variety of gray shadings. Nonetheless, humanity has persisted in looking upon the natural cycles in an oversimplified manner as life or death, ebb or flow, light or dark, good or evil, all to its practical and spiritual detriment. Everything

just simply is, and no amount of philosophical wrangling changes that.

As you ponder this, consider that the One, the Creator, God created everything. With this understanding and knowing, the aspects of life represent where an individual is in his/her connection to that one Source. It is not how good or evil someone is, but rather how closely that person is connected to God, and the degree of closeness reveals the gray shadings between white and black. So, if one is in total harmony with oneself in unconditional love, it can be said that the connection to the I Am is both strong and vibrant, causing that person's light to shine brightly for all others to see. Such a person becomes a beacon of hope to others who are finding their way back to the Source, to the All That Is. In this view of humanity, struggles present themselves in order to validate the paths being walked, and all life's experiences lead to a personal crescendo. Therefore, what you could have deemed positive or negative experiences are actually steppingstones for each of us, steppingstones that illustrate the true strength lying at the core of every human walking this Earth.

Harmony with oneself is of utmost importance when shining light to others. Harmony comes from making peace with what presents itself in order to arrive at newer, higher places. When one creates harmony and peace within self, the entire world changes, because a positive ripple has been created in the cosmic energy flow.

It is peace, harmony, and love that humanity seeks upon this planet, even though it often appears otherwise. What must be realized is that these precious things do not come from others, nor are they the responsibility of others to provide. These things are the responsibility of each individual soul, and when anyone looks to others to stop the fighting or to right a wrong, he or she misses the point of why they are here upon this planet. Every person is capable of being the proverbial lone butterfly that alters everything else in the world for the better. Every person can bring about resounding improvements to this planet.

But, is not up to others to make this happen. It is up to each individual. By making the choice to rise above the pain, the loss, the anger, any one person can create a ripple leading out to all else. And when a relatively small percentage of humanity (some say as little as 10 percent) begin to evolve individual conscious streams, it leads to a so-called tipping point, bringing about a tremendous positive shift in the consciousness of all humanity.

This is occurring now. Many are coming into awareness that what you call higher vibration is necessary for things to change on the planet. This higher vibration can be equated to one's deeper connection with the Source, the internal I Am. This is the path of light, if you need to understand it in those terms. Those who teach of the light versus dark, good versus evil are feeling the shifts that are occurring, and those shifts in human consciousness have been creating a genuine dichotomy, a more purely black-and-white view that actually does reflect the situation. One large group of humans is ascending to higher vibrations of love, harmony, and peace, while simultaneously, another group that aspires to attain enlightenment unfortunately continues to lead fear-based lives with old beliefs that have been handed down through generations and have mutated into areas you call darkness or evil. Fear is what binds a soul to the heaviness in and on your planet, so it is time for those of you who are ready to release those fears to break free so that you may live in unison and harmony with the I Am.

Your story, dear heart, is one of resilience and deep faith, despite your having fallen deep into the darkness many times during your incarnation on planet Earth, and you have been provided steppingstones for any others who are ready to consider walking them. It has been a valiant journey your soul has chosen, and you have never walked alone.

First heal from the words said to you out of hurt and pain, and then dig into your younger years on this planet. Heal those, and we will continue to work through you to share the story of your evolution.

CHAPTER ONE:

Early Childhood

The sizeable second-generation Polish family of nine that I mentioned earlier raised me with strong Roman Catholic traditions and faith. And for the bulk of my childhood, our family lived in the rural (former coal mining) town of Freeland in northeastern Pennsylvania, inextricably bound up in the local parish church named St. Casimir's. Devout Catholicism coursed through our very veins; it bled into every aspect of our lives, and it seemed embedded in the markers of our DNA. As a young child, I thoroughly enjoyed going to church and observing the light beings that would flit around the Blessed Mother. I waited eagerly to see them, for they would not always present themselves, but when they did, I felt such joy and love within my heart, happy to know I was loved by something greater even than my human family. This bond is still with me, but I must admit that I lost it for too many years while I struggled to deal with the aforementioned horrifying turn in my life that created disharmony and disconnection in my soul and with my God.

I have often heard it said that a shaman is either born a shaman or experiences some form of wake-up call whether it be via a near-death experience or death of egoic self to be awakened to the calling. This death might be through a lightning strike, flatlining on the surgeon's table, or as in my own case, an awakening via life trials that broke me down almost completely. I experienced an awakening through life's kaleidoscope of events. These events brought me a shadow space where I began to deeply contemplate who I was before, how I had come to be in a place of brokenness, and by what means I needed to take to become renewed and ultimately fulfill my highest purpose.

I feel as though I've died a few deaths in the course of this one lifetime of fifty years, through some passages that I had a measure of control over and through others over which I had no control whatsoever. This is my journey of who I was, what I felt life did to upend me, and how I eventually righted myself.

The first highly symbolic dream I recall came to me at age 5. In this etheric setting, I saw my maternal grandfather and a deer in a tiny coal patch close to a small bridge over a shallow creek. Grandfather Dziadzia, standing alongside the deer, explained to me that it was his time to pass away, and yet that he would continue to be nearby whenever I needed him. I vaguely remember the melancholy of saying goodbye mixed with the peace of knowing he would always be available, and after I fleetingly looked away then back again, seeing that he was gone but that a second deer stood in his place.

I mentioned having sustained heavy losses of loved ones in my childhood, and a major loss came at the death of my infant sister Stephanie due to heart issues related to Down syndrome when I was but five years. I don't have much recollection about the time that Stephanie was on this earthly plane, but I do remember the pain that enveloped our home afterwards. In a very real sense, I lost not only my beautiful little sister Stephanie, but I also lost my mother, for Mom went into a deep spiral of depression.

The grief consumed Mom, and she locked herself away from reality for quite some time. I remember her crying and running down the cellar steps, closing the door behind her, and locking it. As a child, I didn't understand her grief, but I certainly understood the loss of Mom. I, too, died a bit when Mom wouldn't come up from that cellar.

Thereafter, my sisters, brothers, and their friends seemed to take over as caretakers of me, for I was six years younger even than my nearest sibling, a sister. Needless to say, I have minimal recollections of that time, for as I have mentioned, the brain has a wonderful way of protecting itself. I do recall my much older sister taking me to shop for school clothes, and I remember the store, a dress we picked out, and my feeling of happiness at having that new dress. I felt important having gone shopping with my big sister, and I proudly wore that dress for the school photo that year. Looking back at that photo today, I seem to express happiness in it.

Most unfortunately, Stephanie and Mom were not my only tragic childhood losses. At school, I had a best friend named Michelle with whom I often played and giggled, both in her front yard and at a Freeland public park we two loved. A favorite of ours was the park's merry-go-round, which we would spin for each other for hours at a time, seemingly never tiring of it and never wanting to end our delightful rides.

But during the summer of 1976, it came to pass that we both got off that merry-go-round once and for all. Michelle's life stopped spinning completely, and as a result, my heart broke completely. This occurred at a time that by all rights would have been particularly happy for my family and me, because Mom, Pop, my youngest sister, and I vacationed more than a 1,000 from home at what seemed half a world away at the splendid Walt Disney World in Florida. We drove there from Freeland, and since my parents were antique dealers, we stopped along the way to sell their merchandise.

I vaguely remember Walt Disney World Park, but with crystalline clarity I recall the night in Florida that changed my life remarkably. Within our motel room, Mom was on the phone, Pop had his legs stretched out across the bed, and my sister was over near me on the opposite side of the room where I had just emerged from the shower. Mom hung up the phone and declared solemnly, "Bad news. Michelle's been in an accident at the park, and she isn't doing well."

Somehow, I knew this was inaccurate. Somehow, I knew that Michelle was dead, and I remember accusing my Mom of lying. Subsequently, it came to light that Michelle had died instantly in the public park. The park staff had installed a new sliding board before I had left, and that slide had collapsed then landed on top of Michelle.

I remember the long ride home with my sister sitting beside me, trying her best to extend consolation. I was too locked in my world of grief for much in the way on consoling, and I promised Michelle in spirit that I would never forget her. I remember telling Michelle that whenever a penny dropped, I would think of her.

We rolled back into Freeland on the afternoon of Michelle's funeral, but my parents did not get us there in time for me to say my goodbyes, and I believe their tardiness was intentional. Mom did take me to see Michelle's mother, though, and when we walked in the back door, the poor woman was sitting at the table, absentmindedly staring off into space. I sobbed, and Michelle's mom held me tight. She told me that Michelle had received my postcard from Florida, and she said that her daughter had been so happy I'd sent it to her, because Michelle hadn't thought I would. I was confused. Why would Michelle have thought I might not send her a postcard?

The postcard was placed in Michelle's casket with her and buried that day, a day that changed me significantly. Michelle and I were 10 years old when she died, and I have kept to my word and never forgotten her precious memory. It did take me 14 years, though, before I could bear to visit her gravesite; I went by myself and wept bitterly. Since that first visit, I've returned a great many times, and melancholy still fills my heart with each visit.

After losing Michelle, I became more of a rebellious child in my pre-teen years. One day, after I'd skipped school, Mom pulled me across the street by one ear to the pizza place and queried the restaurant owner, Sal, "Was she in here today?"

I think Sal must have reacted to the look of fear and dread on my face, because he covered for me and said I'd not been there. Years later, I also learned that Sal had a daughter my age, so he must have extended some understanding my way.

I continued to follow my young rebel quest. For example, I smoked cigarettes and talked to earthy boys, some of them older than me by several years. In fact, my first sexual experience was with a boy named Wendel when he was 16 and I was only 12. Wendel had shown an interest in me, and we talked quite a bit at the public park and at the YMCA, which was next to the park. One day, Wendel picked me up in his Chevy Nova, and we went for a ride past Highland, toward Eckley, and then turned onto an old coal road. After finding a good parking spot, we began to kiss and ended up in the back seat, doing it right there like so many teenagers over the years.

I didn't particularly enjoy my first lovemaking, for I was a jumble of fright and excitement, and I could not stop worrying, *What if Mom finds out? She'd kill me.* Well, she sure did find out shortly thereafter by reading my journal account of it. Mom was devastated, mortified, and angry, and I was grounded indefinitely. Wendel's mother was called, and we two youngsters were ordered to stay away from each other. Wendel and I abided by those orders.

I seemed headed down a short road to big trouble, so my parents soon opted to move outside town where they could monitor me more easily. Up until then, our large family had dwelt on the second floor of my parents' business, which was a combination Laundromat, dry cleaning establishment, and antique shop. That property had no yard, but it did include a small driveway on which I'd enjoyed playing ball against the wall of the building and/or heaving a ball up on the roof, which I was able to do on many occasions. The public park that Michelle and I had delighted in so often stood only a few blocks from my house, but after her death I had rarely gone back there. Prior to and following Michelle's death, I had attempted to set up "tents" on our back porch, but that never worked out very well, and I all but lost interest once I assumed the rebel girl persona. Several times before giving up on the porch tents idea, though, I toppled off the porch and had to receive stitches to repair the cuts I sustained, and more than once, those stitches were located on the same parts of my body that had already been stitched from earlier porch tumbles.

So, it came to pass that our family moved outside the immediate town of Freeland, which seemed like an excellent plan to my parents. As they saw it, this would avoid my getting in with the wrong bunch of youth, or continuing with my profligate ways, or tumbling off the porch again in such a way as to cause lasting damage to myself.

The approach used by my parents, and I can appreciate the good sense behind it, was that I would be safer both from my own freewheeling tendencies and from less-than-desirable outside influences. The plan itself seemed sound enough, but like so many things in life, this move to a more wholesome and secure rural home led to unanticipated consequences; specifically, our move there set the stage for the horrifying trauma I have repeatedly alluded to. Little could my parents have guessed that the exercise of their best judgment in relocating me would soon turn out to be the greatest threat imaginable to my well-being, a threat that would rent our family asunder and have catastrophic impacts on the Freeland community at large.

For, at the same time our family relocated from town, a newcomer arrived in our midst, a newcomer who seemed to be God's gift to Freeland, but who proved, instead, to be a plague on us all.

CHAPTER TWO:

Years of Abuse

This nightmarish portion of my story begins in the basement of St. Casimir's Church in Freeland during a class that Catholics refer to as Confraternity of Christian Doctrine (CCD), a class that was led by the new priest in our parish, Thomas D. Skotek. For several reasons, the arrival of this new priest was the talk of Freeland. Skotek's predecessor had alienated many of the young people in our congregation, including one of my two brothers, and with this changeover, my Mom earnestly hoped that my brother would return to the church. In time, this new priest answered Mom's dreams regarding my brother, but ironically, my own soul-fracturing nightmare also began at the very hands of this new priest.

By all accounts, Thomas Skotek was an instant success in our church community, and was frequently credited with having literally "saved the church" from fading away due to attrition of its youth.

Father Skotek quickly renewed community life in our parish. He began the Sodality of the Blessed Mother, Junior Choir, Senior Choir, women's groups, and men's groups. He was involved with the young and old of the church. He went to basketball games and took the kids out for pizza afterwards. His sermons were remarkably inspiring, and those who had departed the church came back in considerable numbers. The people of Freeland simply loved this dynamic priest, and he seemed to love us in return.

However, my long journey into darkness got underway at the first catechism class led by Father Skotek. On that day, the priest spoke effectively and with a pronounced sense of humor about Yahweh, which means "I Am, Who Am" or "I Am Who I Am," and though his lighthearted, jocular approach surprised us youngsters, it nonetheless put us all at ease.

As was typical of our youth gatherings, the boys sat on one side of the room and we girls on the other. I was seated in front on the girls' side between two girlfriends my age, and when Priest Skotek concluded his presentation regarding Yahweh with a final, clever joke, he called our attention to an important announcement at hand. He informed us that girl volunteers were needed to count and record monies from the tithe envelopes collected at each offering, and he concluded by saying cheerfully, "Anyone interested, just raise your hand."

Several of my acquaintances responded at once, for they were obviously thinking, *How cool is this? A hip new priest asking for our help!* A few seconds after the priest acknowledged these friends of mine, I shot my hand into the air to signal my interest in helping and was acknowledged in turn.

Little did any youngster present that day realize this was the beginning of the man's twisted deception of one and all of us, of our families, of our church, of our entire community.

It is clear in retrospect that Skotek's outwardly innocent request for girl volunteers actually amounted to him trolling for eager, easy targets. However, at the time, his call for female assistants seemed harmless, because Skotek then would need to follow up by seeking permission from each girl's family. I don't know if the priest telephoned or actually visited my family home in connection with me becoming a money counter, but what I do know is that my parents gladly granted their permission.

It is only an assumption on my part, but I believe that Skotek's so-called outreach served more as a means of espying each girl's home and family situation. From subsequent events, I also assume that my parents were doubly enthusiastic about my candidacy. For one thing, it was an honor for a member of our family to serve directly in the church, plus my mother and father would have hoped that this admirable work might prevent me from landing in the back seat of another boy's automobile. A third assumption I have made, and I think it a very reasonable assumption in light of all that happened soon thereafter, is that my parents regarded the new priest so highly and were so delighted to have this charismatic, talented, celibate man of God on hand to provide spiritual guidance to their youngest child in particular that they were led to confide in him my having had sex with 16-year-old Jimmy. From my parents' point of view, the money counting position at church would be both a glory to God and a deterrent to any more automobile back seats. As some may say: *An idle mind is the devil's workshop.*

In my case, both parents genuinely loved me. My siblings all loved me, too, but the age range of my siblings was so great that I had already become an aunt by my sixth birthday. By age 10, I had four nieces and nephews. My parents were hard workers who strived to provide us all a good life. They traveled throughout my childhood, with me often in tow, to sell antiques and collectibles at flea markets and antique shows, therefore they were remarkably busy with life. Furthermore, they grieved the early deaths of their parents and of two children who passed quite young. In my parents' busy lives, granting permission to the charming new priest for me to assist with the tithes represented such a grand blessing they did not question it.

I had much free time to myself as a child, playing in solitaire with my Barbie dolls. I had only one close friend, Ruth, after Michelle's death in 1976. Life had changed me after Michelle died; psychologically and spiritually my intuitive gifts were stored in a broom closet under some old photo albums. Trauma changes the brain, but it also does many things to the soul, sometimes transforming it, sometimes transmuting it, sometimes breaking it beyond easy repair.

As I stated earlier, Michelle's death was so heartbreaking for me that I could not bring myself to visit her grave until I was an adult, even though her memory always lived inside me, sweet and kind friend that she was. And as a consequence of my heartbreaking loss, the reader will recall that I'd become a rebellious young girl; I was, as we say, full of piss and vinegar, overly eager to speak my truth and to stand up for what I thought was right, even with my father. After one situation, I spoke out very firmly about a family issue involving an older sister, and never again did Pop intercede with disciplining me. I was not even a teenager at the time I stood up to Pop, and that day's faceoff changed the dynamics of his and my relationship from that point onward. I had forcefully challenged his parenting, and he backed down and away.

I wanted to be seen. I wanted to be loved. I wanted to be a renegade poet whose prose was heard and felt around the world. That was my passion, along with music, and I entered a maverick poem I'd written in a writer's contest, hoping that others would be affected by its message.

Now, back to my account of Father Skotek's recruiting of us girls (between the ages of 12-14) as money counters. The counting sessions took place on Sunday mornings after the 8:30 Mass, at which time we volunteers gathered with Skotek at his rectory. Four or five of us were taught how to sort the money, to put the envelopes in numeric order, and to record individual donations in the ledger. Each of us had specific jobs, and we greatly enjoyed doing those jobs well while listening to music (such as Casey Kasem's Top 40), laughing a lot, and girl talking as only young teens do.

Also during these tithe-handling sessions, Skotek began sharing with us girls various accounts of his life, telling us specifically about his love of the beach, of music, and of God. He spoke kindly to us, with understanding, and he addressed us on our level, all of which opened up interesting conversations regarding Heaven and

Hell, God and the Devil, and everything to do with those weighty topics. Through these in-depth discussions, we learned of God's healing powers, His forgiveness, and His goodness.

Some of us volunteers were selected by Skotek to do additional work within the rectory, such as type the church bulletin, answer phones, and clean the house. I was one of those chosen, and my parents gladly granted their permission for me to expand my tasks.

Sometimes, following the money counting sessions on Sundays, we girls would accompany the priest to the bank for deposit of the collected money, and afterwards, any of us who lived some distance away would be dropped off at our individual homes. On some occasions, Skotek would step inside one of our homes, joking with us, and in that way too I think, narrow down which girls he would choose for longer rides in his vehicles and for alone time to talk about our lives with him. On other occasions, Skotek took us girls out to eat after we'd recorded collections, and after a while, he increased the range of travel up to an hour each way, stopping here or there or running a different errand.

The Poconos was one such dining destination further away. The priest knew people throughout that area from having been placed there by the church previously. Over a period of months, these more distant lunches, accompanied by his growing familiarity with our lives and dreams, grew into an invitation for a "day at the beach" with four of us girls, including my friend Anne and me.

All of our parents gave this proposed beach trip the nod, and why wouldn't they? This glorious man of God who had saved our church was clearly a godsend in their daughters' lives.

All us girls were innocently delighted, for Seaside Heights was the destination that day, and we enjoyed a long, wonderful outing of fun in the sun. But, as I sit here and type these words, I recall the priest presenting me with a two-piece bathing suit on that beach trip, the first of many outfits that he'd give to me. Skotek and his brother Fred, also a priest, had gone on a trip to Cape May a short time before, and Skotek had bought the bathing suit for me then. Hmm. No one thought his gift odd then, not even me. I was grateful that he, an adult, thought about me.

On the ride home from Seaside Heights, we were all exhilarated by the fun we'd had, but we were also exhausted for the same reason. The other three girls sat in back and soon fell asleep, while I rode shotgun to keep Skotek company on the long drive, which seemed fine and fitting, for I had become co-captain of our tithe committee, and I thought nothing of the seating arrangement. In fact, I genuinely enjoyed his and my chats about music, school, and life in general.

So, the return ride homeward was enjoyable and went well *until* Skotek inserted an audiocassette tape into his car stereo and said that he had a special song to play for me by Lobo. After playing the song through, he re-wound the tape to play it again, and he asked that I listen to all the lyrics. (https://music.youtube.com/watch?v=rjBzXreFeWg&list=RDAMVMrjBzXreFeWg) He played this music and more by the groups Bread and Lobo, all love songs, including Bread's "Make It With You," (https://music.youtube.com/watch?v=ndY9yaSwnxM&list=RDAMVMndY9yaSwnxM) and he stated at the end of that song, "Now you know how I feel about you."

As he said those words, he reached over with his right hand and took my left into his. I flinched and withdrew my hand, but then he reached over again and more firmly grasped my hand, holding it tight for the remaining journey home.

My reaction to all of Skotek's incomprehensible behavior can best be described by borrowing a certain expression from the parlance of my age group at that time, and that expression is the sentence, "I totally freaked out."

I didn't know what to make of the entire situation, but I decided to take care of it myself, because my parents already thought I was making such poor choices in my life that they would likely have blamed me for the incident.

The next time that the priest and I worked in the rectory at the same time, I asked to speak to him privately. We went into the seating area of the office, and I told him flat out, "I don't think you should have held my hand. That was wrong, and I didn't like it. Why did you do that?"

I was confused, and I wanted answers, but instead of any meaningful answer, what transpired next only confounded me further. Skotek glanced toward his office – and I suppose in retrospect that he looked to be sure no one else was in sight – then he took me by my shoulders, drew me toward him, and kissed me on the mouth right there in the rectory!

I had meant every word I'd said earnestly, but Skotek artfully shrugged me off with that spooky don't-worry-about-it dismissal kiss, whereupon he ducked into his office and swiftly closed the door behind him.

I stood agog and agasp, not having any idea what to make of either the return trip from Seaside Heights or the events of the preceding minute.

But, I did not run. I did not tell. So many times, I've played this scene in my mind, pleading with myself, *Why did I not tell? What power did he have over me? I was 13, and he was well north of 40. What was happening?*

Well, what was happening was the onset of years of shaping and grooming and sex, along with an evil deceit of everyone else under Skotek's spell. After that kiss in the entryway of his rectory office, he went about as he normally did, exhibiting no sign he'd done anything untoward or even unusual whatsoever. I was shocked and surprised and had much to think about. I didn't want to go back to the rectory, and yet Skotek was so completely reassuring that everything was fine.

This weird approach/avoidance crisis within my troubled young spirit led to a fateful day in which Skotek summoned me upstairs on the pretense that he needed to show me something, to discuss something of importance, or to address God only knows what. I remember being very nervous and scared as I approached, wondering exactly why he had sent for me.

When I arrived at his room, he instructed me to sit on the corner of the bed, which I did, and then he quickly reached out and began to touch me "down there," talking to me while he did it. He said that it was all right. I told him repeatedly that I didn't like it, but he ignored my protests and told me to relax. He said it was okay, and he persisted in touching me through my panties, then searched his way behind them onto my bare skin, and finally, inside me. It was then, in that room, on that day, that he first penetrated me. He ordered me to move over toward the middle of the bed, and he removed my panties before pulling down his pants and underwear, which of all strange things for me to recall were white Fruit of the Loom briefs. Skotek leaned into me, shoved his penis into my vagina, and began pumping.

For me, this motion seemed to last forever, but I think it was actually of short duration. He finished outside of me on the bed, and then told me to get myself together and go back downstairs, directing that I should go down first and that he would be there shortly. And that's precisely what I did. I listened to what he told me to do, and I did not falter. I listened like a child listens to its father, and I followed every command Skotek issued. I still remember seeing Anne downstairs at the typewriter, pecking out the church bulletin and having no idea what had just happened to me.

And no one else at St. Casimir's knew, either. And I never told, even though such abuse was repeated for years longer. The occurrences were more frequent during daylight hours. He would bring me up to his room and draw the curtains. If he heard an automobile or other sound, he would leap up to see if someone was outside, peeking out of the side curtain like an old woman does to spy on a neighbor.

Skotek had me touch his penis. He taught me to stroke it, what amount of tension to apply with my hand, and what movements of my hand to use. He taught me how he best liked his penis sucked, not too hard nor firm. Teeth were a big no-no. And as all of that advanced, so did his exploration of my body: my breasts, my labia lips, my vagina. He explored me with his fingers, he explored me with his mouth, but we had missionary sex mostly with his hot heavy body atop mine, him having me hold his sides while he went inside me. It was horribly wrong what he did, what he had me do, but he skillfully manipulated everything to make it appear all right. He cast what he was doing, what we were doing, as if it were wholly natural, when in reality, it was deeply twisted and perverse. Skotek was thirty years my elder, three times my tender age, and a "celibate" man of religious prominence within the community. People loved and trusted him. Everyone loved and trusted him.

The trips with groups of us tithe-collecting girls became more frequent and expanded to greater distances. Skotek had deeply embedded himself within my family, within my home, within my friends. He had embedded himself within my church, my place of calm, my place of connection with God. He had embedded himself within my school, both on the board and within the classroom. He had embedded himself within my entire circle of friends.

The first overnight trip that we all went on was to see REO Speedwagon in Madison Square Garden on July 10, 1981, at which time I was 14 years old. My parents were selling antiques in Brimfield, Massachusetts, and they had wanted me to accompany them, but Skotek talked them into allowing him and the other girls to come pick me up in Massachusetts so that we could all go to the concert together. And that is what he did. He drove up to Brimfield with Anne and another of the girls to pick me up. I remember that night drive to New York City vividly, because Anne sat in the front seat, unlike on most trips with me sitting

27

in front, and I remember that as we rolled along toward the concert, Skotek reached around and behind his seat to caress my leg. The other two girls took no notice, both because it was dark and because they were tired.

We girls all had a great time at the concert, and what teenager wouldn't? From that outing onward, the trips snowballed in number and frequency and are something of a blur to me. That first trip to New York City was swiftly followed by additional jaunts back there, to Philadelphia, to the Jersey shore, to Boston, to Notre Dame, and to Toronto.

There were many concerts to be seen, many shows to attend, many artists and venues to enjoy, and so many beaches to visit. Whatever artists I or the other girls wanted to see, whatever beach we wished to visit, I was given Skotek's credit card to arrange the trips. We sometimes ventured to Philly twice in a week, and these trips were typically overnight outings in which we'd stay at the hotel near Veteran's Stadium (the Vet). As mentioned before, there were trips to the Jersey shore where we stayed in Wildwood many times at the Adventurer Hotel right at the end of the boardwalk. The priest would give us all money for the rides and food, and he also provided alcohol. Later, he offered cigarettes for any of the girls who wanted them.

Skotek took me to bars with him, and I'd have drinks. No one would know that he was a priest, because he'd wear blue jeans and, typically, a T-shirt, leaving his clerical collar behind. And I would go to the Atlantic City casinos early on with him, having no issues of age. The girls and I loved the band The Hooters, and we went to a nightclub in New Jersey to hear them one night, underage.

It was an exciting time with all of these travels and events, but of course there were always the dark, underlying sexual secrets.

These trips were too numerous to count, whether they were day trips, overnight, or extended. New York City trips occurred right after Christmas for one or two nights, and we would stay in the city in higher end hotels. During those times Skotek had his room, and the girls and I had ours. When in New York, we never toured museums and such, but rather we shopped, dined, and were shown a more luxurious side of life. Fantastic restaurants were frequented by all of us, including Tavern on the Green where I met Anthony Quinn. We had seen him in the Broadway play "Zorba", and I was in awe of meeting such a talented man. We had also seen Raquel Welch in "Woman of the Year" during that same time frame. I remember that the musical "Cats" was still in the planning stages when we began taking trips, and I was amazed to learn that the theatre was to be painted black for the production. Another trip included "Evita", which became one of my favorites, and afterward, the girls and I learned many of the play's song lyrics and sang them in unison on road trips.

I think I resonated on some level with Eva Perón, the poor, misunderstood girl on the rise.

There were breezy trips to the shore during the week in summertime, the winter trips to New York City for Broadway plays, fine dining, and shopping. There was a trip to Boston simply because we had never been there. And there were innumerable trips to Philadelphia for concerts and so much more. It all seemed perfect from the outside. Even on the inside, it came to feel all right in time, as odd as that may sound, because the predator priest's abuse had become so normalized. Me sleeping in bed with Father Skotek while at the beach somehow seemed "normal."

It was a tangled mat of mind games that each of us participated in so that we could rationalize all the partying and fun without facing harsh truths. For example, I remember a trip when Father Skotek's niece, who was close to my age, joined us at the beach accompanied by a friend of hers. Well, Father Skotek made a dramatic point of mentioning that he always slept by himself, ever playing the celibate priest role outwardly and ever meeting with success at having others bend their minds to suit the alternate realities he conjured.

My girlfriends could see what was happening, and they questioned one other, yet they never spoke to me about it, and they practiced their own versions of this mind bending in order to dodge guilty consciences and to avoid putting a halt to our delicious excesses. To this very day, the three others that made up our original group of girls have not spoken about what happened during those years, at least not with me.

I enjoyed beach trips most of all, and we very often stayed in Sea Isle City, New Jersey, in summer, coming back home to Pennsylvania for the weekends so that the priest could say Mass. The Spinnaker in Sea Isle City was a condominium that a former parishioner would let Father Skotek use as a getaway, and it was beachfront with a sprawling master bedroom having its own bathroom, plus there was a splendid deck off the living room. A second bedroom was near the entrance door, across from the kitchenette. The girls would usually sleep in the second bedroom or in the living room, and Father Skotek and I slept in the master bedroom. Often, though, I would sleep on the balcony where I was free to watch the sunrise by myself, and as best I can recall, I sometimes slept in the living room when other girls and/or family were present. Of course, I can only write about what I remember; some old friends recall another girl sleeping in that master bedroom whenever I slept on the balcony, and though my memory on this is vague, I have no doubt it is true. What passed as normal for my friends and me back then certainly was not normal in any aspect of that word.

Life was both good and terrible at the same time.

Already in my young life, a clear-cut schism in my soul was evidenced in the ongoing sex and luxury within the illicit, immoral, deceitful, and bizarre relationship with Father Skotek as opposed to my sincere and devoted service work in our community throughout high school.

On Monday nights we volunteers would travel to Kingston to teach mentally challenged individuals in the Confraternity of Christian Doctrine program (also known as CCD). On Saturdays we would teach adult mentally challenged individuals at White Haven Center. To me, these outreaches were more than mere community service, for they represented an extension of my very heart. They entailed working with my friends, choosing lessons for Monday that would carry through to Saturday. They entailed committing time with my friends to share that Jesus and God love us and make us each individually unique.

I was also involved in a Catholic political club in high school, and we all went to Washington, D.C. for the annual March for Life. Yes, my friends and I marched on Washington, D.C. to highlight the ongoing Roe v. Wade showdown, and as the reader might readily guess, we were staunchly Pro-Life.

That unflagging stand we took on behalf of the unborn made subsequent events in my life all the more tragically ironic and soul-splintering, because near the close of my junior year in high school, I took note of some telltale bodily clues and made an appointment for myself at Planned Parenthood. Predictably, the pregnancy test was positive. I was a pregnant rising high school senior, almost certainly carrying the illegitimate child of our popular, celebrated church priest, the fraudulent, disgusting, molester of a priest who had vigorously promoted piety even as he had vigorously sown perversity.

I wrote "almost certainly carrying the illegitimate child of our popular, celebrated church priest," because some small measure of doubt existed due to yet another perversity of this unwholesome man: Throughout my high school years, Father Skotek had directed me to date boys near my age and to be intimate with them, obviously to distract any attention from what he was doing to me regularly. The point is that I had sex with other partners during high school because the priest insisted I do so. Father Skotek said that I would be like other teenagers with a normal life. Well, there had been nothing normal about my life under the control of that man; it was a tortured double life that Father Skotek had guided and controlled, a tortured double life that had led directly to pregnancy.

What, oh what, was I to do under these bizarre circumstances? The counselor at Planned Parenthood said, "Your options are to keep the baby, to put it up for adoption, or to abort, but you do not need to decide yet." It was a tremendous decision, and the staff provided me with pamphlets in hopes these would help guide my decision.

I know that I told Father Skotek as soon as possible, and I believe I did so immediately after my appointment. I clearly recall that he and I did not discuss my pregnancy off to the side that day so long as we remained in the company of my friends during a senior pictures photo shoot at a studio in Exeter, Pennsylvania; Father Skotek drove all of us there, and there was no opportunity to broach the subject of my pregnancy until much later in the day.

By the way, I found it quite ironic that my senior photo was taken the very day I learned the deceitful priest had impregnated me. Whenever I now look at the photo taken of me that day, I see a beautiful smile, but I remember the dread of the unknown behind that smile. So painful to remember, so painful.

There were two versions of my pregnancy, one rooted in harsh immoral truth, and the other in a new and cruel deception designed to conceal that immoral truth. Version One, The Truth: I was 16 and pregnant, almost certainly by the church priest who had abused me for years without using condoms. As I've indicated, though, there was some small doubt about the patrimony, because this weird priest had directed that I date young men my age and be intimate with them to assure that no one would suspect or learn what went on behind closed doors of the rectory. And what went on behind those locked doors (with a new security system) was that he had regularly mounted me in unprotected sex month after month, year by year, leaving little question about who'd fathered the child in me near the end of my junior year.

As soon as we had arrived back in Freeland from the photo session and were out of earshot of my classmates, Father Skotek immediately declared there was no question of me keeping the baby. In fact, I was to get an abortion without any consideration of keeping the child or even of giving it up for adoption. Father Skotek convinced me that abortion was the only choice, considering that I was about to become a high school senior bound for college. He asked what a baby would do to my plans for college, and then immediately answered himself that it would mean I wouldn't be able to go. Next, he posited that it would break my parents' hearts. My mother and dad would be crushed he went on, because they had high hopes for me to be their first child to attend college.

In short, Father Skotek manipulated me after abusing me and almost certainly impregnating me. Father Skotek had already made the decision for abortion, and I followed his decision and guidance obediently like I had done on his bed for years, like an obsequious concubine. And even though this ran directly counter to my personal beliefs and to the teachings of my church, I did what he had chosen for me to do. I accepted his reasoning in place of my own. I accepted from him that I had no option to keep the baby or to give it up for adoption, because there would be too many questions. Too many people wondering.

I was young. I was terribly scared. And I was already groomed and conditioned for this subservient existence I led under the thumb of Father Skotek, the troubled priest who controlled me and handed down the order that I undergo abortion post haste.

So it was that I came to be standing in the office at the front of Father Skotek's desk while he wrote out a check from the church account to cover my abortion. To conceal the check's true purpose, I believe that he made it out to "Cash."

Speaking of concealment of truth, speaking of intentional deception, this brings us to the other version of my pregnancy that I mentioned, a mendacious and cruel deception that I call Version Two, The Deceit: A young man that I had dated named Sam was led to believe that he definitely fathered my baby, because Father Skotek decreed it would be done. And the priest dictated that only Sam and my friend Anne would be fed the line about Sam being the father; no one else was to even know of my pregnancy at all. It still aches in my heart that, to this day, Sam believes as a certainty that he was the father of the child, and I sorely regret having this man believe I chose to kill his child because I'd decided on my own to do so. My soul cries out in an echo of Sir Walter Scott's great quote, "Oh! What a tangled web we weave, when first we practice to deceive."

The day came for the abortion, with the plan that Anne would drive me to the clinic in Allentown and back. That was the plan, anyway. I remember so clearly the clinic and the cold blankness of it, the questions prior to the procedure to verify my wish to proceed, and the information about the method to be used. Of course, I was already aware of the procedure; I had studied this, I had determinedly marched for life, and yet there I sat, awaiting an abortion myself. Anne and I simply sat and waited. The room was grey with no sense of feeling, at least not to me. Then, my name was called, and I walked to the assigned room with the nurse. I remember going into the room with its bare walls, white sheet, stirrups… and machine.

In moments, it was done, and I insisted on driving us back, despite the agreement that Anne was to have done so. I needed to take some kind of control, and me driving was something I needed just then. My parents were away, and that night Anne and I slept in the rectory. I slept on the bed next to Skotek, and Anne lay on the floor next to my side of the bed. In the days that followed, neither my pregnancy nor abortion was even mentioned by Skotek. As far as he was concerned, it was all over and done. But I wrote. I wrote about it. It was certainly not over and done for me, and I journaled about the pain and loss I continued to feel. It was my release, a partial salvation for my sanity.

Not long after my abortion, a group of us went to the beach, staying at a Sea Isle City condo that we had always gone to during the week. On that fateful trip, I was in the "sun closet" developing my tan when Skotek chanced upon my journal and read my unfettered agonies about the lost child and my attendant grief. Then, he literally ripped those pages from the journal, screaming that I was never to write about this again. "Don't you ever tell anyone about this! It's over. It's done."

I cried to be in the room with a man who wanted me to forget about something that I had done only because of him, having no other viable option, and all as a result of his years of molestation.

All this time, the other girls stood in the doorway, watching him shout, and if they knew what he was shouting about, none of them ever mentioned it. What's more, my writing came to a halt, except for two poems and this recollection, here and now.

I entered my senior year, and outwardly at least, exhibited no signs of the sexual abuse, pregnancy, or abortion. A few months later, however, a girlfriend became pregnant and wanted to get an abortion because she was fearful of her parents and what they might say. Skotek, as priest of our church, guided her to talk to her family, and he arranged to facilitate the conference. I remember that on the day of the meeting, I was in the rectory and asked Skotek why not let the young woman get an abortion, given that he had unequivocally demanded I get one.

I got no spoken answer from him, only a stern, silent stare as the side bell rang. In fact, he never answered me, and my friend gave birth to and raised her baby, an option that Skotek had denied me.

Consequently, my grief and truth were buried deeper yet. I drank, partied, and masked the pain; I went to school drunk, but no one noticed. Something had changed inside me on top of the changes from the sexual abuse, and in late November of that year, I appeared to attempt suicide with an overdose of pills, not enough of them to actually kill me, but enough to signal a clear cry for help. I remember, as the movie reel plays inside my mind, calling Skotek from the phone in the laundry room and telling him that I'd taken the pills, and him knowing that they were not a lethal dose. I don't remember what else he said to me on that call, but I can still remember the pain and brokenness I felt.

After this, I had my first (and last) counseling appointment at Catholic Social Services (CSS), and they let me know that I need not return. Did Skotek have a hand in that? I think he must have. I think that he persuaded CSS he could counsel me through my mental health crisis, and they allowed it. Where, oh where, were the trained professionals at CSS?

Years later, in post-marriage counseling with my second husband, the therapist told me that CSS had suspected Skotek was doing something inappropriate, but that they had had no concrete proof. Seriously? They could have stopped it all then and there. As it was, they did nothing, and the abuse continued.

But how could all of this have taken place without early detection, and what aspects of my early life led me to be so compliant in this troubled man's web of sex and domination? I think it best that I make some attempt at a satisfactory explanation by simply relating aspects of my heritage, family life, and dreams as they come into my memory.

And for some reason, the observance of Easter and all that it meant in my childhood has presented itself as a good starting point. I'm remembering how Good Friday was always a day of no meat, no phone, no radio, and no television between the hours of noon and three o'clock, which we held were the hours that Jesus Christ hung upon the cross. During those hours, my family members took turns grinding horseradish with an old hand cranked mill attached to the edge of the countertop. The idea was that the stronger the horseradish, the more tears flowed, and the more tears that flowed, the greater clearing of our sins. It was an absolution of sins through physical means, at least in Mom's way of thinking. But as time went on, that tradition slowly vanished and was supplanted by church services during the Easter season, spending hour upon hour praying, dramatizing biblical scenes, and singing songs such as "Were You There (When They Crucified My Lord)?"

My father was once one of the twelve selected to have his feet washed upon the altar at Easter, a high honor for him. Quite ironically, Dad's honored feet washing came by way of the very priest who was sexually abusing me.

I have so many memories around those church services, and all of us girls who shared the many concert trips, the beach outings, and the shopping excursions with Skotek felt a powerful familial bond within the church community and services as well. I suppose that in both settings, we were very much like a family unit that traveled together, and like all family units, we had an almost unspoken hierarchy with Skotek as father, my very young self as a mother figure, and my girlfriends-classmates as the children. Come to think of it, what a bizarre, twisted sort of family, but a family of sorts, nonetheless. And I never had looked at us in these odd roles until I read what my friends wrote in our yearbooks; phrases like "Thanks, Mom" and "I'll miss you, Mom!" hit a note of disgust as I realized the perversity of such thought. Had Skotek been aiming to create some makeshift family all along? It felt so creepy and unimaginable, but perhaps there was an established name for his weird desire to conjure a family all his own.

We four girls who most often traveled with Skotek called ourselves the Four Musketeers, comprised of Anne, Cindy, Renee, and me. "One for all, and all for one," we'd say. And however unnerving it was for me to admit it, or to come to terms with it, I had been the mother hen all along. Everything that ran smoothly did so because I'd taken charge. When the other Musketeers got drunk, I took care of them. If one or more of them wandered away with a boy they just met, I found them and brought them back. Whenever they fought with one another, I stepped in to restore calm. I had willingly participated in a macabre, make-believe family with a complete fraud of a priest. I felt despicable as well.

And that leads me to the topic of traditional family and to them being the most important people in my life. Growing up as the youngest of seven, there was a vast age difference as I've stated before. I've always said that I am the youngest on one side of the family and the oldest on the other, with one side being my siblings and the other being my nephews and nieces. My extended family loved spending Easter Sunday together eating Mom's ham, along with kielbasa and paska bread.

And on Christmas Eve, we celebrated a traditional Polish Christmas meal called Wigilia. Then on Christmas morning, my brothers and sisters with their families would come over to eat, and the kids would open gifts that Santa had left them. I thoroughly enjoyed Christmas, and because I worked at the church, I was able to purchase nice gifts for the kids such as velvet dresses from Wanamaker's in Philadelphia. I loved viewing various storefronts and going into shops to see what I liked for my nieces and nephews or myself.

But this pleasant set of memories brings me, as has so often been the case in my life, directly to shopping and clothing memories of a very dark nature from the time Skotek stole my innocence. One of the first outfits that the priest bought for me was a red plaid skirt that came well above the knees, a red wool sweater with my initials embroidered on it, and matching knee highs. In hindsight, that was a schoolgirl look that particularly appeals to pedophiles, but at the time, I was clueless as to its perverse, selfish significance, and I suppose that Mom was as well, for she never questioned it nor blinked an eye.

As time went on, and as the priest began to provide me money for my own shopping, I had to spend within reason because he provided each of us girls an equal amount to avoid suspicion. Skotek often mentioned that if the other girls stopped coming, he could buy me more things and take me more places, but I think he never discouraged them, though, because that, too, might have drawn unwelcome attention.

I've come to realize how craftily the man proceeded, making no decision without careful scheming on his part, but until recently, I'd not recognized the extent of his guile. As I think back to the places that he took me around the community, it becomes clear that he had duped everyone else as well. For example, he took Anne and me to be fitted for our first contact lenses, and I can remember hearing the doctor's assistant say that the priest had done this because Anne and I were poor and needed help to obtain contacts. Consequently, the eye doctor gave huge discounts on the contacts for both of us, never realizing that our families were not desperate, but that Skotek had used this as a means toward his self-serving, perverted ends.

Within the same town, Skotek took me to a jeweler to select items that I liked. I pointed them out, and then they were gifted to me at Christmastime or on my birthday. It makes me wonder what Miss Kosko (the jewelry store owner who was also a teacher at my school), thought when she saw the priest bring me in to choose favorite pieces, or later, when the priest returned to purchase them. What might have happened if she had brought these oddities to the attention of the school principal or of the local police? She never made any such report that I am aware of, but would that have possibly ended Skotek's preying upon children years earlier?

I also wonder what my English teacher, a Mr. Fulton, was thinking when I submitted material from my journal about the abortion as part of a graded assignment. Mr. Fulton, one of my teacher's, simply taped the pages of my journal together and wrote upon the front something to the effect of "Be careful what you write in here." There went my help and rescue.

Throughout my years in the Catholic school system, Skotek was always there. He was on the school board. He was an instructor; he was my instructor, and I remember him teaching about the various forms of love and the different personalities. He told me that I had a sanguine personality. Other people did notice the sporty vehicles that he owned (a van, a Camaro, and a Cadillac), but no one seemed to think it odd that I drove his brand new Camaro on so many occasions or that Skotek often commented how good I looked behind the wheel driving it. The man even taught me how to drive, first in an unoccupied area of the Wyoming Valley Mall parking lot, and then on the Schuylkill Expressway with my friends in back, praying for their safety. He took me for my driving permit. He took me for my driver's test.

Skotek even gave me his class ring from Michigan State, but he sharply instructed that I keep it out of sight. He took me to his relatives' houses. On Sundays, he would often spend the afternoon eating dinner with my parents and me, followed by games such as Uno and Rummy. He became a solid family fixture, and my family had no issues with me going anywhere with him. They trusted the priest implicitly. I don't understand how no one put two and two together, or why no one questioned the activities in the rectory.

I was closely connected to my various family members as a young girl and in my teenage years. I had nephews and nieces who were only six to 10 years younger than myself, and I was involved in my older siblings' lives and in the lives of their children. One of my sisters ventured to the beach in summer with the priest, my girlfriends, and me. She suspected nothing. My parents and I went to the beach with Skotek, and they suspected nothing, either. One of my brothers was quite active in our church, as was his wife. They suspected nothing.

I remember days of spending time with Skotek and my family members during the holidays, at which times he often presented me with elaborate gifts. Still no suspicions. One Christmas, the priest gave me a diamond necklace, and on another, a heart-shaped garnet ring with a diamond on either side. Skotek gifted me choice perfume, fine clothing, and top-end radios. At Plymouth Meeting Mall, he bought me a beautiful Himalayan cat that I had fallen in love with, although I did have to give it away when I arrived home with the pet, because Mom said I could not keep it.

To some people, looking in from the outside, it may have seemed like I thoroughly enjoyed my life during high school. In the main, I was neither sullen nor withdrawn. Instead, I was most often vibrant and happy with my friends, and time spent with them was, indeed, delightful. We laughed, sang, danced, swam, traveled, and had fun. Plus, I was always lending an ear to someone who needed it, for I was the go-to friend, offering sage advice to my peers.

Yes, from the outside looking in, it likely appeared that my life was splendid, with no appreciable woes.

So many firsts that were milestones in my teenage years were with this debased priest, making the whole relationship so much uglier and unfortunate. While from a distance it may have all seemed wonderful, behind doors there abounded grotesque secrets. Secrets that rent my soul. I remember him holding my hand as we drove on trips in the night. He did this often while the other girls slept in the back seat. He would always be on guard in case they stirred and would pull his hand away quickly any time they did. However, if the girls slept soundly, he would spell out on my palm "I love you." He would sign letters and notes to me "PAT," standing for *Puella Agape Theos,* which is Latin for 'girl, I love you'. Such twisted thinking for a man in his forties who claimed devotion to a life of celibacy to his God but lived a life devoid of venerable deeds with young females. I was a young teenager, and there he was, spewing words of love to me like some adolescent schoolboy. I admit that it made me feel special. It made me feel loved. It made me feel important. And I guess this perverse man knew precisely what I longed for, what was lacking in my life even at that young age.

This priest had carefully considered how to get what he wanted. I remember now when he first brought condoms to use for sex, which as best I recall, took place after my pregnancy and abortion. I remember his agitated, nervous behavior, his stashing them in his nightstand next to the bed on the right-hand side, the side that he slept on. He kept a great many condoms in that nightstand drawer, he made a point of teaching me how to put them on him, and he used them regularly after the abortion.

I asked him one day where he obtained the condoms, for he was too well known in the area and couldn't simply stride into a pharmacy and purchase them. He told me that late at night he would drive to a White Haven truck stop that had a prophylactic machine in the men's room. I remember him telling me of it with such excitement in his face and body movements, and he seemed to be quite self-satisfied that he'd carefully avoided being seen after saving quarters for the condom dispenser.

Another means by which Skotek manipulated circumstances to meet his own ends while masking his moral bankruptcy was having a "security" system installed in the rectory. Skotek told others the alarm system was for the safety of the money counters and general security, but it was all about his own safety, his own security system to let him know when someone who had a key was entering the rectory. The days of him peeking through the side of the window curtains to see if anyone was outside were gone. He had acquired an alarm that would warn him when someone might find him out, so he relaxed and then abused me with more complete abandon and frequency.

Once this security system was in service, Skotek did not have to worry about anyone coming in and catching him with me. The alarm could be set so that the unarmed interior detectors monitored the outside perimeter, and he would know if someone used the passcode to come in as well. So, with this reassurance, the sex fiend had his way with me in his bedroom more times that I could

45

count. It was most often during the daytime whenever I cleaned the rectory, worked the books, etc. So many times, so many times that I don't choose to remember for the sake of my sanity and for the sake of any loving relationship I might have with another man, which brings me to a vital aspect needing to be spelled out here and now: in the hundreds of instances of Skotek using my body, sex never had an element of sacredness to it. Sex never had an element of passion to it. Sex was always a "hush, shh, don't tell." Dirty little secrets kept behind guarded rectory walls with no one looking in and no one asking questions.

The man was a twisted genius in how he arranged tasks. I was the household manager for the rectory, and all laundry was washed, folded, and put away by Anne and me, including bed sheets. Everything was dusted and vacuumed by her or me. It required a great deal of forethought on his part to get me alone all those hundreds of times and to have molded me into actually thinking that my subjugation and molestation were normal.

And it did become "normal" in a sense. The deceit that Skotek layered upon me became a norm. Even conversations with him regarding boys and dating were intertwined with the sick relationship he imposed on me. After having directed me to date boys so that no one would suspect or discover what he was doing, he would question me how the dates went and if there was sex involved; he wanted to know everything. The hellish priest had such control over me that I did whatever he requested every time, even though it violated everything positive that I thought as a young girl a relationship might be.

Even though mom was fully aware of the sexual violation with Wendel, I think that she chose to ignore it, perhaps as a form of cognitive dissonance as her own type of coping mechanism. Mom had always counseled me to save myself for marriage, explaining that sex was a beautiful thing between two people who love each other, devoutly love each other, and saying that I was too young yet to understand and have that kind of love. I think that she had hopes for a different life for me. I saw my older siblings in relationships, but they were much older, and I didn't see the relationships in their homes, plus my parents did not display tenderness publicly. I don't ever remember my parents hugging or holding hands, for in front of others, they were busy doing their work and businesses. They supported each other, yes, but I never witnessed exchanges of kind touch between them.

So, in reflecting back, I had no good relationship models early on. Through my tortured years of high school, Mom faithfully heeded Skotek's suggestions. She would not have gone against his advisement, and he knew that. He had her wrapped around his finger, and he was acutely aware of what he was doing: infiltrating to keep his secrets hidden. And as my high school years rolled on, Mom and I argued increasingly, but Pop never stepped in. Mom took to writing letters of her hopes for me, of the potential she saw in me, but she also invested considerable time in describing what a tramp looks like, inferring that I matched those descriptions. That injured me badly, and yet, Mom had no way of knowing that her implicitly trusted priest was the very source of all that she objected to and worried about in this regard. That is to say, even as Skotek violated my body on countless occasions, he encouraged me to dress in a floozie-like fashion in order to attract boys (plural) and to have sex with them (plural). How could Mom have known that I was merely doing what the sex-obsessed priest directed me to do?

Whenever I re-read Mom's letters now, I can feel the pain in her words trying to grasp what was happening to me, what was going on in my life. She never knew until much later after it was over.

In reading my own journals now, I sympathize with one very confused little girl searching for love and never finding it. It was always my romantic notion in those pages that someone would sweep me away from it all. No one ever did, and though it is usually quite painful to read entries I made so many years ago, at least those pages offer understanding as to what my mind, heart, and soul were enduring. The words written there were eagerly searching for something that I never fully felt until now, as a much older woman; it took me three ended marriages and two live-in boyfriends to realize that what I actually needed all that time was self-love. As a child, I did not understand this, of course, and that marked me as a prime target for the perceptive pedophile priest who came to our town ostensibly to save the church. I think Mom felt that she could save me as well by providing a pious, secure, safe haven by way of Skotek. What an irony!

Another ironic twist is that Mom forbade me to join any sports teams throughout grade school and middle school, most likely in fear of something terrible happening to me. But that's just it, for something terrible did happen to me, and it did so for years on end, right under her and Pop's watch.

I wanted to take ballet and I tried once, but Mom would not let me continue. She never said why, and I never went back. I also attempted to play basketball in junior high, but Mom would not let me do that either, for it would have meant regular practice sessions away from home and bus rides to games. In ninth grade, I had interest in color guard. Again, Mom said no. She did not trust leaving me to anyone, except Father Skotek. Consequently, sports were not in my history growing up.

Considering Mom's highly protective stance in keeping me away from team sports and school spirit, I wonder what she'd have thought had she known what took place one day at the rectory when I asked Skotek why he had several cheerleading outfits hanging in his clothes closet. Skotek's means of answering me was to instruct that I put on one of them so that he could take photos of me in the outfit, which was in the church's uniform colors of red and white. So, although I was never allowed to join the grade school and high school sports teams, and though I never served as an actual cheerleader at school, my cheerleader image was immortalized in a highly suggestive manner standing upon the bed of a demented Skotek, the very person my Mom entrusted to steer me toward a clean and upright life in the grace of God.

I didn't realize I had lived through such pronounced depravity under the control of a pedophile until I was free of him by virtue of going away to college. I am told that it is normal, what I felt, due to traumatic bonding. That is remarkably creepy, right?

Right.

CHAPTER THREE:

Turning Point

The improper relationship between the priest and myself continued long after the abortion, but things soon dramatically changed once I graduated high school and matriculated at Marywood University in Scranton, Pennsylvania. During my freshman year, Skotek would still drive up to visit and take me to dinner, or he would call to ask how things were going.

In February of my freshman year, a pivotal event happened. "I believe it saved my life."

For Valentine's Day, Skotek came to campus and presented me with a dozen red roses, this at a time when the price for them had skyrocketed to more than $100. Oh, if only I could turn back the hands of time, I'd have refused those flowers on the spot, and I would have paraphrased one of the notable characters (Meggie Cleary from *Thorn Birds*) quotes of "Take your bloody roses! Roses have thorns that prick and tear." The television miniseries based on the novel of the same name was wildly popular at the time this situation unfolded in my life, and come to think of it, in a strange sort of way, I was a living extension of Meggie Cleary.

Even though I cannot turn back the hands of time to reject Skotek's inappropriate gift of roses, or any other of his many inappropriate gifts for that matter, something did occur that Valentine's Day to positively redirect my life and give rise to renewed hope. You see, the exorbitant cost of roses that year had been a frequent topic on radio, and my floormates at the college dorm found Skotek's gift both excessive and peculiar, and they had no qualms about speaking up to say so. My floormates' startled reactions and feedback are what first enabled me to recognize the scope of what had happened to me, and as best I recall, a college girlfriend named Dana then suggested counseling for me because of my obvious depression and whatever else she had astutely perceived in my situation.

What a blessing Dana and her recommendations were, and I recently reached out and heartily thanked her for suggesting I get help back in that freshman year at Marywood. I believe that if Dana had not done so, I would no longer be in the world.

So, off to my first official counseling session I went at the Victims Resource Center. This proved to be the first of a great many therapy sessions throughout college (and beyond), and I do not know how I was able to complete my coursework while simultaneously lifting my emotional sluice gate. Quite bluntly, I had to acknowledge that throughout my teenage life I had been devalued, demoralized, and victimized by a priest who still continued to serve Mass as if he had done no wrong. Those times were excruciating for me. I drank too much, I partied too much, and I did too many drugs, all to dull the pain and memories, and all representing a familiar carryover from the drinking and drugs of high school. I was foolhardy as I self-medicated in a fruitless attempt to make life more tolerable and less real.

At that time, I was also decidedly loose and free with my body, which was definitely not treated as my temple back then, rather, it was just a vessel for someone else's pleasure, not even for my own. I loathed myself, yet I continued my unending, vain search for love. Life was a too-swift revolving door of school, sex, therapy, alcohol, and drugs, with one or more of these taking preference over others at various times.

That period of my life I am not proud of, for it clearly revealed the dark side of me and a lack of respect for my body, my spirit, my soul. It was a battle to even continue living. There were many times that I thought killing myself would be the best thing. The deep, painful sorrow would finally be gone. I'd finally be free. But wait, the Catholic church, my church taught that if I killed myself, I would not go to heaven, and I certainly didn't want to land in purgatory or hell. I felt I was already dwelling in those horrid places, anyway, and I didn't want to prolong it any more than absolutely necessary.

Yet there was many times after high school that I just wanted to check out, to make the memories end, to make the awful feelings of self-hate and self-destruction go away. I can't tell you how often I pondered leaving it all behind and the ways that I would accomplish the task. I am thankful that something or someone always pulled me back to reality. I came upon a quote by Dag Hammarskjold in college, and it inspired me to keep going, to never give up: "Life only demands from you the strength that you possess. Only one feat is possible; not to run away."

Throughout college, my classes were tough, and my studying was tougher yet at times. I remember being in the throes of self-pity and severe depression when I met once with my academic advisor, Dr. Bisset. She listened intently to my plight, but then bluntly declared that I had become responsible for myself and the course of my life, so it was time to act like it.

I was taken aback and angry at first, thinking how dare my advisor say this to me. Doesn't she realize what I've gone through? How can she be so callous? Well, Dr. Bisset, I want to thank you for that live-saving realization. You were absolutely correct and spot on. It was the very thing I needed to hear to catapult myself out of despair, to continue my studies with determination, and to take more meaningful steps to healing.

I went on to graduate from Marywood University, and later, to obtain a master's degree, not letting the abuse I'd suffered define me or bring me down, even though it did temporarily knock me to the ground many times through the years. I have always gotten back up, stronger, wiser, and healthier of mind, body, and spirit, and Dr. Bisset's gift of straightforward honesty and wisdom represented a critical turning point in my life.

I am delighted to report that Dr. Bisset's rousing wake-up call yielded even more benefits in my life. In addition to my resolution to buck despair, to forge ahead with my studies in special education, and to take those more meaningful steps toward healing, I also recognized that all my miseries over the years had been tethered to my stifled silence. So, if I wanted to make real progress in overcoming my past, my hang-ups, my heartaches, I would need to find my voice and tell my story.

I had never told anyone else of the abuse I suffered as a teen-ager. I had wanted out of the rectory, and I had attempted to break free many times through the years, but my parents would never allow me to quit. Yet, I still had not revealed Skotek's sick secrets in all of that time. I weathered in silence Mom's worries that I had become a tramp. I endured, without outcry, the bizarre sexual molestations of a man thrice my age. I belittled myself, without speaking to anyone about it, when Skotek steered me into dissolute sexuality with various boys. I tortured my soul without shouting it from the rooftops when the priest insisted I kill the child inside my womb. Yes, I choked all of this and so much more down. I suppressed the truth both literally and figuratively. The chokehold on the very core of my being had led to absolutely nothing fruitful in more than five years of hellish torment.

Dr. Bisset was precisely right. I was responsible for the course of my life, and it was time to act like it.

The time had come for me to speak.

CHAPTER FOUR:

Taking Stock, Taking Action

I resolved to reveal everything to Bishop Timlin, which was the correct and proper way to handle Skotek's willful, sustained abuse of church authority and resources. I was confident my revelations would result in Skotek being removed from any position involving underage parishioners, and I hoped it would also lead to him undergoing evaluation for aberrant behavior, both sexual and otherwise. I made this resolution in the midst of juggling my difficult college studies and my numerous therapy sessions, so I had to crease my brow and carefully schedule the trips back to speak with the bishop in order to see through my commitment to the truth.

Bishop Timlin heeded what I had to say most carefully. He took notes. He promised that the matter would receive careful attention, and he referred me to a therapist other than the one I was already seeing at Victims Resource Center. I was decidedly optimistic, and I appreciated Bishop Timlin's reference as well. Furthermore, the bishop reassured me in short order that Skotek was being sent for evaluation to a professional facility in Maryland. *Wow!* I thought. *This is going very well. I should have spoken up years ago!*

My optimism and confidence were not well placed. The professional facility in Maryland was in fact a church-run enterprise, sharing in common the interests of the diocese, the powerful Catholic churches in the USA, and the Vatican. The official report issued by this facility concluded that Skotek had not violated me at all, and the rationale for this conclusion was based on Skotek's having repeatedly claimed to love me in some misguided way. In other words, the report found there had been no sexual abuse since Father Skotek said that he believed I was his true love.

Say what?

Atop this crushing setback was Bishop Timlin's endorsement of the report and his subsequent decision to transfer Skotek to a new position at St. Aloysius Church and school in the nearby city of Wilkes-Barre, Pennsylvania. I did not know it at the time, but Skotek's new position was at a church that included a school! I protested what I thought was a simple transfer to a non-school church, but my protests and pleadings were ignored and nothing further was done. With each of my requests for meaningful action, I waited longer than I should have in hopes that good sense would prevail, but it eventually became obvious that I was, in the language of New England hunters, barking up an empty tree.

By that juncture I'd passed my 20th birthday, and I had to gird my loins for an altogether new resolution. I had decided to turn Skotek into the secular authorities, specifically to the Luzerne

County District Attorney, Robert Gillespie. I lived with my boy-friend Ron at the time, and I asked his mom to accompany me. She agreed at once, so I gathered my plentiful evidence of letters, cards, photos, and journals, then she and I drove down to Wilkes-Barre from Scranton that day. I remember being extremely ner-vous about going to local authorities outside the church, but I kept in mind that I needed to be strong and that the abuser charlatan named Skotek had to be stopped.

I remember waiting to be received in the district attorney's office at the county courthouse with what I'd brought, and then, once I had been called, I remember giving the detectives a rather detailed account of what had transpired with the priest from 1979 to 1984. I gave them ample information regarding how it started when I was still 13 and was transitioning from eighth grade into high school. I explained to them that he'd been brought to our church in an effort to reverse the exodus of young people, but that almost immediately, the trolling, grooming, conditioning, and sexual abuse began. I told quite a story, and I endeavored to tell only that which I could clearly remember as a solid witness.

And of course, I handed over my wealth of corroborating evidence. There were the photographs Skotek had taken of me standing in that cheerleading uniform on his bed in two sugges-tive poses; there was my journal, unsealed from the tape that my English teacher Mr. Fulton put there when he'd warned me to be careful what I wrote and shared; there were the many cards Skotek had given me signed "PAT" and "Sko," with Skotek's inappropriate handwritten words of love added; and there was much more yet.

The detectives dutifully took down Skotek's name, my parents' names and addresses, and I don't remember what else, and then they told me they would investigate rigorously and get back to me. In the meantime, of course, Skotek was serving at another church in close proximity with the school children there, and he was there only because Bishop Timlin had stubbornly insisted Skotek had not violated me.

Soon after my revelations to the detectives, they questioned my parents, and I came to know through roundabout means that Skotek had told my parents what he did with me, and then my parents shared this information with the detectives. It is anyone's guess how Skotek framed his *confessional* to my parents, or how they then passed it along to the detectives, but I venture to guess it amounted to more of his thinly veneered Lobo love song balderdash, perhaps it was something along the lines of I loved her so much that I stumbled from grace. Along the same lines of my musings or suppositions is that perhaps it ran along the lines of getting out his Lobo color-by-numbers easel and paint set to depict it as something similar to, "We loved each other so much that all reason flew out the church window."

In any case, it happened that Skotek's brother Fred, the fellow priest, died while this investigation of Skotek was underway, and a lady detective assigned to the case, who happened to be from Skotek's new parish, actually convinced the district attorney's office to give my abuser time to grieve his loss before even being questioned about his sexual encounters with me as a teenager. Saints preserve us! What kind of twisted logic was that?

And, heaping misery upon misery, the district attorney at this time did not once contact me, and my liaison, for goodness' sake, was Ms. Church, the female detective so attuned to Skotek's needs.

During this time, I became depressed and anxious, for this was the second round of frustrating sidesteps, delays, obscurations, and distractions preventing Skotek's villainy from coming into the full light of day, and all of it taking place after I had finally drawn myself together to step up and speak out.

Stymied again.

Detective Church kept offering up excuses for delay. And more excuses. And phone calls to her were sometimes not returned. Repeatedly, I got the brush off, and this treatment of the victim (me) as an annoyance was typically accompanied by a remark from detective Church that the time to prosecute was short due to Pennsylvania's statute of limitations.

My response to her inane statute of limitations remarks was, "Well then, all the more reason to prosecute promptly!"

"Well, we would only be able to charge him with…"

"Okay, so charge him already."

What followed each of these exchanges invariably were more lapses and runarounds. I often wondered if, behind the scenes, the county officials lacked the will and the confidence in taking on anyone associated with the Catholic Church, even someone like Skotek with an obvious disregard for common law. My gut instincts were that the district attorney's office would never charge this man (I believe they never got around to questioning him directly), because it would cause too much media hype and too many questions about the Catholic Church at that time.

It is important to keep in mind this took place in the 1980s.

Slowly, but surely, this lethargic inaction on the part of detective Church and the other district attorney staffers steered me back to new meetings with Bishop Timlin and renewed attempts to have him properly investigate and/or discipline Skotek. I was so afraid that other youngsters would become victims of Skotek, and I am certain my fears were well founded, but I simply could not manage to get Bishop Timlin to take appropriate action.

Fast forward for a moment some 20 years later when one day at my job in Wilkes-Barre, a school psychologist was talking with me and offhandedly mentioned some concerns she had about a young girl who attended the church and school where Skotek had been transferred. I felt that something had to be done at once, for it seemed quite likely this girl was Skotek's latest victim, so I wracked my brain for a means of shaking Bishop Timlin loose from his fixed position.

The oddball solution that came to me involved outright lying on my part, but I could think of no other way to break Timlin's inertia, and what's more, this oddball solution of mine actually succeeded. Out of complete exasperation and desperation, I composed a letter to Bishop Timlin opining that Skotek would never again behave inappropriately with a youth were he to be transferred to a school-less church of his own. In other words, I provided something of a "cover" letter for Skotek, the bishop, the diocese, and the church at large, even though I did not believe for a moment what I'd written myself, but it had become obvious to me that the church system wanted to cover its backsides before taking any appreciable steps to discipline Skotek.

At last, my continued pressure and, more importantly, my insincere letter of confidence in Skotek, resulted in Bishop Timlin relocating Skotek to another position, this one in Mocanaqua with no accompanying school. Skotek last served as a Catholic priest in that church, but from there he was defrocked and lost his priestly status after another of his victims (one who happened to have been before me) came forward with compelling evidence.

Skotek's removal made the evening news in April of 2002, and I wept with relief the day he was finally rejected, although I was also heartsick for any other young people he'd violated in the meantime. Surely there were many others both before and after me, and I wondered who they were. They almost certainly included the girl I knew as "Crackers," the girl who came down to the beach with us on one or two occasions and whose father owned or worked at a car dealership in Kingston. It also includes some who wish to keep their personal lives personal, such as one who was fondled by Skotek when she had her period. And they included many others that grieve me to even imagine.

In 1989, I made a grave mistake in my naiveté by signing a non-disclosure agreement in exchange for a cash settlement. Put another way, the church effectively bought me off for a mere $90,000 and then intended to squelch my newfound voice for all time. I was much too young, and I was under far too much duress to have signed such a document, but I did sign it all the same, and I mistakenly believed it gagged me for many years longer than it did. The actual duration of its effectiveness was greater than a decade, but then (without my knowing of it) Catholic bishops met in Texas in 2002 and voted to null such secrecy-binding agreements. I was made aware of this during the meeting with the deputy assistant attorney general in September of 2018.

Bishop Timlin never extended an apology to me. Timlin never told my parents that he was sorry, or that he had sympathy for the sexual abuse I endured. He never expressed empathy for the shame that my parents, siblings, and I felt. Bishop Timlin, it is men like you, ruled by money, that Jesus drove from the temples as described in Matthew 21:13. Perhaps it is time for Christ Consciousness to walk through and cleanse the temples once more. And Bishop Timlin, there is no gold under your buildings or in your Vatican; the gold is located within our Creator's unconditional love. This 'gold under his building' is in reference to a statement Bishop Timlin made under oath during a court proceeding when asked why he was in the courtroom testifying. His response, I was informed by the family member of the attorney who tried the case, was along the lines of "because (individual) feels there is gold under my buildings". He failed to acknowledge the sexual deviations that were being tried in a court of law.

In the midst of all these swirling events, emotions, and eventualities, I began therapy in Clarks Summit with the therapist Bishop Timlin had recommended to me (I think her name was Adele), but I only went there a few times before returning to the Victims Resource Center in Scranton. I found the care at Victims Resource Center to be very supportive and helpful in my healing process, and as I navigated therapy, I continued my fulltime college studies and a focus on special needs education. My grades did suffer, and I had to retake a class or two, but I had the unflagging support of my mom and of Pop's sister, my dear aunt Julia.

Aunt Julia was my godsend and someone I could aspire to emulate. I loved her spirit and her knowledge. She had an internal, independent strength, and her example helped brace me for the next phase of my roller coaster life, a phase that I often refer to as The Aftermath, which is a reference to the overwhelming aftershocks most abuse victims experience in the wake of abuse, aftershocks that might go on for years, for decades, or heaven forbid, for the remainder of one's lifetime.

CHAPTER FIVE

The Aftermath

Victims of abuse find that the aftermath of what he or she has endured adversely affects almost every area of life. I offer up the following examples to illustrate how far-reaching and deep-rooted is this invasiveness, but please keep in mind these are only some of the great many examples that could be discussed. This vital chapter will cover serious damages done to Trust, Friendships, Family Ties, Faith, Pro-Life, Intimate Relationships, Physical Health, Parenting, and Equanimity. It is my wish in discussing these to foster greater understanding of the traumatized individual who has experienced a pattern of abuse in his or her life.

Trust — I have a difficult time trusting people based on what I've experienced in my life. Do you remember that Michigan State college ring Skotek had given me to have and hold (albeit secretively)? Well, he later claimed that I had stolen it from him while routinely cleaning the rectory. This weird betrayal, added to his years-long abuse, contributed to me losing trust in almost all my fellow humans, and only now as I compose this memoir am I beginning to re-establish myself within small circles of select acquaintances and friends.

And what is trust but an understanding that one has the best intentions in mind, heart, and soul for another? At birth, trust is innate. We trust that food will be provided. We trust that shelter and security is always at hand. As an innocent, trust is established among family connections, and that often becomes the norm for future relationships, but I lost trust in everyone, including my family members. I trusted no one, not even myself. During my teen years and the abuse, I had put my trust in someone, Father Skotek, but that trust was ill placed with so many lies upon lies and deceits upon deceits. My life back then was a living lie formed by deviant deceptions from that priest, and my life took a great many twists and turns throughout my adult years because of this deception and being shaped by it in my formative years.

My heart cried out for love, yet I pulled away and hid in the shadows of my fears of not being enough, not being good enough, not being smart enough, loving enough, honest enough. My life still begs me to trust in others, yet I find it challenging to do so with so much debris left behind in the rubble of my heart. I've had many doors open to me with opportunities to build relation-ships based on open communication, and yet ever and anon, I demanded whole truth from others then only shared with each what I thought was necessary or that he/she could handle. I never revealed my true self to anyone, until lately, but then I opened the floodgate and had no filter whatsoever. What I strive to do, what I absolutely need to do in this regard, is to strike a balance between blunt truth and tactful, gentle words and actions.

Friendships — While in high school, I had many acquaintances and a group of three friends with whom I was very close. We ate together in the cafeteria at lunch. We traveled back and forth to school together, except for one girlfriend who attended another school. Those years in high school, even through the abuse, provided sustaining friendships that have eluded me ever since, probably by subconscious choice.

Studies consistently find that abuse dramatically alters the lives of the abused. I attest that it does by way of so many darkened avenues: perhaps via unspoken secrets or whispered words between and among others, so that among my dear friends of the high school years silence now looms. Anne, Cindy, Renee, and I watch each other's lives from quite a distance, yet I never jump in, and I have never asked any of them if they too were abused; perhaps that would be too painful for me to acknowledge either then or now.

I believe that the mind has powerful means of protecting itself, and sometimes the protective shield can later be lifted, sometimes it cannot. I do know there were grand times down at the beach lying in the sun or visiting Philadelphia, New York City, etc. The world – our world – had so much to offer. We girls had one other, the trips, the concerts, and long discussions about God, boys, and everything else in between. I remember frequently going to one fine restaurant outside Atlantic City. The wait was always long, because it was so popular, but the wait was well worth it for the Golden Cadillac Cocktails, French onion soup, and the splendid seafood. In short, we friends lived the high life of fine dining, great hotels, and grand trips here and there, but not once did any of my friends inquire if something was going on with the priest and myself, not once. That stark fact clearly illustrates the power in perversity, a force so strong that our mind finds a way to block it out as if it did not, nor does not, exist.

When college rolled around, we friends kept in touch the first year, but our contact dropped off sharply after that, and once I began therapy, nearly all girlfriends from high school and college drifted out of my life. As this process took place, not one of us referenced the times that we had, either good or unsettling. Was it too painful a subject for them as well? I often wonder how everyone is, and I spot him or her on social media, but we exchange only a casual click here or there with no real soul meaning behind it.

So, regarding friendship, chalk up another aspect of life heavily damaged in the aftermath of Skotek's abuse.

Family Ties — When the time came for me to reveal the horrible secrets, my father actually blamed me. He told me that it was my fault. Mom blamed herself for trusting the crooked priest. She felt responsible for what happened until her dying day, literally. As for my sisters and brothers, we never completely healed. One of my brothers wanted to kill Skotek; however, that brother endured so much criticism that, instead, he eventually stopped talking to me. I think it was perhaps out of pain of what had happened. (Hereafter, I shall refer to this brother as "my estranged brother.")

My estranged brother's daughter, my niece, posted on Facebook about the priest and the abortion in such a hurtful light to me that I disowned both of them, feeling they'd never taken the time to understand me nor the situation. I lamented that it's easy to point fingers, but it's hard to understand and hear the whole truth. I am happy to note, that same niece reached out to ask forgiveness, and I gladly extended it, so she and I are each learning on this path of life, but it has taken a number of years to overcome that break. The healing continues.

My other brother and his wife outright blamed me for the priest's abuse, saying that I'd enticed him and was the cause of everything that happened. In subsequent years we slowly mended some of the damage this inflicted, and yet I think deep down in our hearts much of the schism remains.

Regarding my four sisters, not one of them has fully healed. One says that she frequently agonizes over having not realized what was happening to me, and she beats herself up for that. (I will hereafter refer to her simply as my "guilt-ridden" sister to assist the reader in following along.) Another of my sisters feels that Karma will come back to visit Skotek one day, and the other two never even speak of what took place with the priest.

When my father died, we were going through photos, and when an image of the priest turned up in one of the photo albums, my guilt-ridden sister thumped the image with her finger and quickly flipped the page in disgust and anger. The priest's name is never stated among us; instead, we circumlocute it.

The family turmoil in the wake of revelations about Skotek's abuse extended far beyond just my relationship with other family members, for it created wreckage among their relationships as well. My father's decline and death provided heartbreaking evidence of that. In the months and years prior to Pop's passing, he called for two family meetings with us children, but only five of seven attended. With mom passing a few years earlier, the first meeting regarded what Pop wanted should he become seriously ill, and this included a directive against any life support and details of what he wanted to wear at his funeral, what type of funeral it would be, and where the funeral breakfast would be held. It also included financial aspects of his estate, or what was left of it by then. Each of us siblings was to choose what he/she wanted from the house, and when it was time, we were to take it. It also included who would have first dibs on the house itself. The second meeting was in the early fall when Pop decided that he would go ahead and sell the house, and then move out

Well, for this deeply intimate determination by us family members, I received no phone call or text from any sibling, but rather a formal invitation by mail.

My estranged brother was called and informed of my father's progressing illness over this period of time, and when Pop became sicker, a sibling called that brother's daughter to inform both of them through her, but my estranged brother never answered his phone for any one of us. The day Pop died, I was the one who called and had to leave a message on his telephone answering machine. He never even came to say good-bye to our father, and I was profoundly bitter.

I did not understand why my estranged brother made no showing whatsoever, that is, I did not understand for years, until the very day that I was writing this portion of the book!

I had called my guilt-ridden sister to ask if I could visit her for a much-needed break from my home life. When I arrived, she and I began talking of Pop's house, of all that had transpired in and around that time, and I told her I had begun to write this book. She expressed to me that not one day goes by without regretting her failure to see what was happening to me almost in front of her face. "How could I have been so blind and trust that man?" she asked-not expecting an answer because there could be none.

At that point she happened to mention the fractured relationship between Pop and my estranged brother, and she asked if I knew why that brother had stayed away even when Pop had faded and died. When I told her I had no clue whatever, she explained that it harked back to one of the many days the priest spent at our house, specifically one on which he'd brought along gifts for Pop and me, and one on which my soon-to-be-estranged brother also dropped by for a visit. After the priest departed that fateful day, Pop and his visiting son got into a heated argument regarding not only the gifts themselves, but Skotek specifically, for my brother had sensed something was seriously amiss and found the gifts inappropriate. My father, in turn, told his son to mind his own goddamned business, and that if he couldn't comply, not to let the door hit him in the ass on his way out and not to ever come back.

Oh, God, so that's what happened! My estranged brother, who tried to speak up and protect me, was exiled for it. Furthermore, as a direct result of him and his family not being welcome at my parents' home, my protector's children grew up devoid of either paternal grandparent.

I am devastated. I disowned the very person who stuck up for me so many years ago and who had to pay dearly for it. Now, I join my guilt-ridden sister in asking, "How stupid and unknowing could I have been?" But I cannot erase time. I do not know where to even begin apologizing to him. My heart is broken. And what else might be out there that I do not know? What other deep secrets were kept from me or were buried deep in my soul?

My fellow guilt-ridden sibling also told me that I had been in the house that day. I do vaguely remember it, but as I have said before, one's mind is powerful at repressing trauma and keeping itself shielded. I struggle with knowing that it is past time to unlock the doors of my cluttered mind and to sweep the cobwebs out.

I often wonder what my family ties would look like today if the abuse had never happened to me. I see where my family members have landed and how their lives are. I wonder if we would still be a close, connected family in some way, without the abuse. Every family is complex, for at times you unquestionably love the others, but at other times can be certain you hate them. Perhaps you choose to live without them, yet you lament their loss.

Some of my once-close siblings ended up leaving it to me to reach out to them after the revelations of my abuse. In my mind, I know that makes sense, but in my heart, my inner child is screaming out, *Please take my hand! I'm scared, and I feel alone.* And alone I remained for years because my stubbornness took over and the agony of being left again lingered. I know that I am an adult now, yet part of me longs for the greater sense of belonging that I felt early in childhood. There were so many judgments put upon me by my blood family that I built a shield of protection around myself that I would have loved to knock down, yet fear kept it up. The fear of rejection of love was and is real for me, and I believe that it evidences itself in an ugly variety of ways. Too much solitude. Long distance friendships. Acquaintances that are casual. Why build relationships when people stop loving you, anyway? This is what the abuse did to me, and it affected everything in my life.

Faith — As a young girl, I loved God deeply, and I delighted in attending church. I had a particular thrill at witnessing heavenly spirits fly about inside the church, and I eagerly hoped for their appearance without a trace of fear. At a very young age, I embraced my spiritual gifts of being able to see cherubim and seraphim and of having insights and intuitions attuned to the divine, but my molestation by Skotek created a black wall that distanced me from my faith for many years.

To the casual observer, this black wall and loss of faith would not at all have been obvious, because I continued to participate heavily in the church throughout my high school years, singing in choir, studying with keen interest the miracles, praying earnestly, volunteering for various outreach programs, and of course working all four years in the rectory. Furthermore, it's not that I lost my faith altogether in God's higher power; up to and including my college years, I still turned over my sorrows, losses, and pain to God in gratitude. However, my faith was clearly conflicted, confused, and otherwise compromised in all of those years by the complex web of deceit and immorality foisted onto my young, impressionable being. As part of this struggle of my soul, I stopped attending Mass most of the time, finding that I could not reconcile the hypocrisy and pretentiousness of Skotek.

Most fortunately, for the sake of my spirit, there were some positive role models during that time in the church. For example, I chose to attend a charismatic service in which healing was incorporated with the program, and the priest leading that service was genuinely pious and loving. His devotion exuded from his very essence, and when he lifted the chalice during presentation of the Eucharist, I saw a stream of gold manifest and knew that God and Jesus were present within that host priest. Thereafter, even though my faith was severely shaken overall, as I've shared, I felt a powerful connection with the Holy Eucharist, and I never stopped receiving it whenever I did attend a Mass.

Pro-Life — Abortion is not something an abused woman can easily forget, even if she tries and even if she calls upon the considerable capacity of the mind to block undesirable memories. The issue of abortion is raised on medical forms. How many pregnancies? How many live births? With each new doctor's intake that needs this information, it is recalled. For me, it is recalled each and every February, and it is remembered deep inside my being. It is recalled every time I speak up to reveal what happened to me, attempting to spare others the kind of abuses I suffered. And it is brought to the fore any time other people choose to share details of my story, either with or without my permission and with or without my knowledge they are going to do so. And it was most certainly an excruciating issue to cover with my children, suddenly and unexpectedly, many years after the abortion itself.

In short, this aftermath from my years of abuse is an oft-occurring and deep-seated agony.

Intimate Relationships — One does not easily or quickly recover from the trauma of sexual abuse and then settle into a warm, healthy partnership, even if the recovering person is quite blessed to have attracted a genuine, tender, caring partner. Instead, recovery is usually a long and arduous process in which meaningful intimacy is, at best, elusive, but more likely is apt to make the recovering person's body and soul actually cringe, just as it did previously when abuse took place. One's neural, emotional, and spiritual wires get tangled, and illogical reactions take place, and there are so many avenues related to healing after sexual trauma, with intimacy being a big black dot on a white wall. And that big black dot does not go away by being ignored, either.

I am certainly not proud of my sexual past, for it often amounted to *Wham, Bam, Thank You, and maybe I'll answer if you call.* Years of sex with Skotek wedged disturbing sexual associations into the crevices of my mind. I often wondered if I could ever have a "normal" sex life. What's more, even if that proved possible, I questioned whether I could remain faithful in a relationship, especially with so much deceit in the way I was steered during my teenage years. Sex did not equate with a feeling of mutual respect and attraction. Sex was more of a tool, an activity that numbed my senses and aspects of myself that I foolishly and fruitlessly tried to forget.

There was always a long list of potential triggers for me during sexual relations. A smell. A particular touch of a hand. A certain motion or look from a lover. Any of these could instantaneously render me frigid, wanting nothing more than to have the intimacy end.

The reader might well ask how I maintained any intimacy in my adult life, especially when I reveal that I have already been through three marriages and several live-in arrangements. Well, much of the answer is contained within the question itself, because the collapse of these many relationships owed in no small part to my myriad torments regarding intimacy.

It is important to say that I passionately loved my first husband, Pete, but even with him, my desire diminished far too quickly. Ironically, another great problem that developed between him and me was that I strongly wished to have a child, but Pete was not at all ready for fatherhood at that time, and he said so flatly and repeatedly. In other words my interest in sexual intimacy was sharply waning, and yet, I was championing sexual relations to insure that I'd get pregnant. I was so determined to have a child that, even though I loved this man with all my heart, I left him.

The aftermath from sexual abuse can and does lead to all manner of jumbled disasters.

When I divorced Pete, one of my best male friends from high school, a man named Jim, came back into my life. Jim and I had never been intimate in high school, and though we were just once during college years, it had simply been a one-night stand with no further import. However, in the wake of my divorce, we two repeated our college tryst, this time I became pregnant. I was indeed scared in the situation, but was very happy about being pregnant. I knew in my soul that I should not marry Jim, but I heaped on another jumbled disaster and did so, anyway.

This second marriage was more one of friendship for me than anything. Although I did have a love for Jim at the time, I do not believe I was ever in love with him, and although he and I had two daughters together, there proved to be far too little keeping me married to him. I'm sorry to admit this so bluntly, but it is my truth.

I then wed a third time and in this marriage I diligently attempted to work through intimacy issues and share a healthier sexual relationship. There were many times when I engaged in self-talk during our intercourse to reassure myself so that I could stay loving and positive. For example, I'd remind myself, *This is your husband. He loves you. He will not hurt you. You are an adult. You have control.*

Any or all of these words were what I might say to myself during sex and intimate moments with him. It was as if I had to give myself permission to enjoy sexual pleasure freely in my mind, body, and spirit. But there were plenty of times I was unsuccessful with this, despite my earnest efforts. Sometimes, I needed to stop. Sometimes, as he made love to me, tears rolled down my face when I involuntarily recalled what had been done to me in my teenage years. Sometimes, I successfully employed a neuro-linguistic technique known as cancelling out a memory, using *Cancel. Cancel. Cancel,* Or, *Swipe Away!* Or, both terms. Sometimes, I just wept and was held lovingly in his arms. He was patient with me during those times, and I am thankful for that.

We had a son together. Nonetheless, my marriage to him also ended, and the specter of sexual abuse followed me into my years as a single mother of three children.

In the midst of one relationship, I sat down with pen and paper then poured my heart out in a particularly raw, but revealing, entry. I believe it serves well to illustrate how abuse crippled my attempts to form or maintain any positive, intimate relationship:

"I think that I shall stay in this relationship that I have now.

Not because I wholeheartedly want to, not because I feel that I can give 110 percent (because I know that I can't), but because I am so unsure of what I want for myself for the future. I have the opportunity right now to say, 'No, this relationship is *not* what I want.' I will not say that though. I have had so many losses in my life already. I do not want to start again, and fail again. I don't want to fail again, and I believe that sums up how I look at my relationships. I feel that I have been a failure at keeping relationships, both friendships and intimate. So, fair warning, I am poison, stay away from me. I will grab your heart and tear it out and stomp on it like a bunch of grapes in a barrel. Seriously, even if I thought that my Prince Charming was right down the street (which I think he may be), I would be wary of developing another relationship."

What a pathetic thing!

"Part of me just wants to be alone, just alone. But then, I think of what I want. I want someone that I feel passionate about in more ways than just lust. I want from a relationship the desire to be with someone, think about his kiss, and think about how I feel when he holds me, when he is not around. I did not have that in most of my relationships, but I experienced the possibility and know that it can be a reality. I know that I once did have that feeling, but it is so long gone, and I am unsure I want to work to get it back. I want someone who makes me laugh and makes me smile. I think that our relationship is too damaged for him to bring a smile back to my face. I look at him and see how he is trying to change and to work to make this work. I see how he looks at me. I heard the optimism in his voice when we were planning our weekend getaway. I hear how he says that he loves me and waits for an *I love you* in return, not to hear it. I see the pain in his eyes. How long will he last with me not telling him that I love him? How long will he wait for me to make up my mind? How long will he hold out with me holding out? How long is it fair to make him wait for me to make up my mind?"

So, I did manage to enjoy intimacy as an adult, but not with any consistency. My success changed like the weather. Sometimes I allowed my body to be used, and sometimes I used my body as an emotional release valve. Sometimes hot, sometimes cold. Enjoyable and despised. Countless times I have either cried or stifled tears during intimacy. Soul shattering and disheartening.

I always sought to be positive within a relationship, but I struggled with the actual sex and my body. Eventually, I did manage to relax more often and at least enjoy my partner and our connection, body to body, but even then, it was not spiritual for me.

Sex was never a spiritual act as I now believe it is intended to be. I'd never viewed sex as a sacred act of raising a man's conscious and healing his soul until decades later, and that is one pitiful reflection of me as damaged goods from Skotek's abuse.

Physical Health — Through the years, I have had numerous medical issues related to the sexual abuse and the emotions retained in the walls of my body, my structure. Nightmarish cell memory has generated pains that made me feel as though I had cancer and would surely die. My uterus has been removed due to tissue massed around it, surely owing in part to blocked feelings and negatively charged emotions that built up internally over time. I have dealt with piercing pelvic pain that comes and goes, connected with various memories, and vaginal pain that stabs like a knife, but that too is rooted in psychological malfunction, my gynecologist tells me. And there are other psychological, non-medical phantom pains in parts of my body caused by the trauma of years past. To make matters more severe, the medical prescription for these pains involves nerve blockers and anti-depressants, and I have had to take one antidepressant over an extended period of time and have had prescriptions for anxiety medications as well. I am currently glad to be antidepressant and anti-anxiety medication free, but I was grateful for their use when I needed them the most.

These physical ailments sometimes combined with psychological stresses in bizarre, debilitating ways. For example, when I was married to Pete, I became paralyzed by a deep fear of driving a vehicle. I simply could not drive long distances by myself; going through tunnels and over bridges brought on insurmountable anxiety. Imagine a little woman sitting stiffly, perpendicular to her seat, hands clenched, and white knuckled grasping the steering wheel… that described me, but in my 20s. At least I was able to drive short distances locally, but even then I stressed until arriving home. Over time I have managed to overcome this phobia, but for a number of years it held a place of importance in the list of crippling items from the aftermath of abuse.

Parenting — Until they were nearly grown, I never told my children about any of these things I am writing upon these pages, and even then it was forced upon me, as you will see. The subject was out of the question for me. I only gave the youngsters tidbits of information from those years of my life, feeling that they did not need to know. Besides, I'd have had no idea how to talk to them about what happened to me. So, they did not know about all the trips here and there. The shopping. The fine dining. The company that I kept.

Speaking of shopping and of my children, here is quite a twist: as a teenager, I loved shopping, but as an adult, I loathed it, forcing myself to shop for clothes only when the need was great. Consequently, I never had bonding time with my kids through shopping adventures. I think my brain linked shopping to the mental and sexual abuse that I'd endured as a teen, or perhaps it was a disbelief in my self-worth and my self-value. I always strived to give all that I was able to give despite my illogical hang-ups from the abuse, but I am sincerely remorseful for not providing my girls with some enjoyable shopping trips or salon visits or some other girly excursions, and I realize I've left a blank place in their lives because of it. Sometimes my best efforts fell far short of their hopes, and I humbly acknowledge this. I never failed to love my children, but perhaps my silence for all those years of not telling my secret life has made an ugly, indelible mark on them. I hope that as time passes, they might understand my reasons, but for now, I sit on the sidelines, picking up the pieces of long past yesterdays in a grief that I have diligently been addressing in my heart. Perhaps I will have to forgive myself and realize that no parent is perfect, nor is any one person.

I am my own worst enemy at times. I tend to be excessively hard on myself and strive for some crazy internal perfection I can never attain. But yet, I realize it should be fine for me to be imperfectly perfect. Such conflict within my own being at times, with internal tremors at the thought of simply purchasing a piece of clothing for myself! So many moments behind dressing room curtains with self-talk like, *You're safe now. You're an adult, and you're safe trying on and buying a blouse that you like and want to wear.* It has been a drawn-out process, and I am thankful to those who purchased clothes on my behalf because they understood the harsh internal struggles I faced.

Another fracture in my parenting of my three children, whose names are Julianna, McKenna, and Quinn, involves senior year photos. When it came time for Julianna's senior picture, I could muster no enthusiasm at all. I had no photo from the session hung on display in the house, and I didn't even know when McKenna had her senior photos done. I was absent. I was absent for both daughters' significant school milestone because I had traumatic memories of my own.

Julianna, McKenna, and Quinn are my life force, driving me forward to strive and do my best; however, for most of their lives, the aftermath of the abuse I had experienced led me to consider myself broken. As the children grew, I always felt that I needed to be put back together again, that I was not actually whole in the way I presented myself to be to them. As a third example of my parental paralysis, the kids had to deal with me being hyper vigilant about their care. I entrusted them to precious few caregivers, and even family members met with my skepticism and careful scrutiny, especially as regarded my daughters.

Here is another sad example of my dysfunction in connection with adult/child relations: A very near and dear family member became happily pregnant, but due to complications, she had to make repeated emergency room visits before ultimately suffering a miscarriage. I did accompany her on those emergency room visits, I did sit with her, and I did feel her grief overtake joy as her pregnancy failed, but I was walled off from her by having walled off my own experience and telling her nothing of it.

Mother's Day came that year, and I felt her renewed pain, yet she said nothing, nor did I. I wanted and longed to reassure her that the days get better and that one day she would likely be a mom herself, but I was frozen. My mind whirled around telling her. I remained silent. My grief and silence blocked me from sharing life experience to help her heal. Then, the due date of her miscarriage came around, and again, I did not reach out with how she might cope with the day. How could I advise her when she had no inkling I'd lost a child, too? The big secret. The big, heartbreaking, soul-scouring secret that I held locked inside of myself. And though this family member was not my own daughter, my incapacitation at her time of dire need serves as a powerful indicator how compromised my parenting skills were by way of the abuse.

Equanimity — An abused person finds it nearly impossible to maintain a steady demeanor, especially in the face of innumerable "triggers" that jolt him or her back to memories of the abuse. That is to say, an abused individual struggles to exhibit the virtue called equanimity.

This fact nearly slew me during the heavy media coverage of the Jerry Sandusky investigation, a child sex abuse scandal at Pennsylvania State University where Sandusky served as an assistant football coach and was alleged to have molested underaged young men over the course of 15 years. This investigation, and Sandusky's subsequent convictions on 45 of 48 counts, fired salvos of triggers at me, pommeling me one after the other much faster than I could absorb any of them and threatening to unravel the life I'd painstakingly managed to build.

I strove to hold myself together for the sake of my children, but I probably frightened them instead. Also, I had been happily married to my third husband at that time, but I became newly and acutely stressed by the fusillade of revelations about how skillfully Sandusky groomed and manipulated his victims. The similarities in the grooming style between Sandusky and Skotek were so remarkable that I wanted to vomit.

I felt as though I were repeatedly slammed squarely in the face by a succession of airborne bricks.

I had thought I was past my trauma more fully, but the Sandusky revelations smashed that cozy self-assessment and sent me reeling. At that point, I started therapy with a psychologist I had known for years, and seeking the help proved timely in multiple ways, for not only did I face the fierce resurgence of my past demons, but I also had a number of other stressors come up around the same time. For example, McKenna moved out to go live with her dad, my father became weaker by the day with lung cancer, and as I mentioned, my theretofore joyous marriage to my third husband became heavily stressed when I succumbed to the rapid-fire Sandusky triggers.

Then, to make matters far worse, a lack of trust on my part reared its ugly head in the direction of my very trustworthy husband. In a turbulent frenzy, all the emotions and remembrances of my abuse came rushing back to me in crazy ways at crazy times. For instance, one eve I was lying in bed beside him quite peacefully, when suddenly I realized with panic that I lay on the same side of bed that I had slept on with Skotek. I freaked out and summarily insisted that my startled husband switch sides of the bed with me. Anyone in a relationship can understand how glaringly weird my demand seemed; to this man, it made no sense, even after he realized my urgency stemmed from things that had happened a number of years earlier. The incident unnerved me as well, although I was the one who'd abruptly clamored for the swap.

While he grappled with my strange behaviors, and while he sincerely attempted to be understanding and patient, I continued to work full time, to rear my other two children, and to attend regular therapy sessions.

Then Pop died, and a few months after that, we faced a situation, which irrevocably wrecked our marriage. So, as stated earlier, after a trio of fated marriages, I became a single mom again. But even more stressors soon beset me. During the time of the children and me moving, re-adjusting, and settling in, I was diagnosed with atypical lobular hyperplasia with pre-cancerous cells identified. Not long after that, I completely lost my voice and developed a barking cough.

Life was falling apart, and so was I.

Safety for my children and myself was critically important to me, and I, lacking anything that could be said to resemble the virtue of equanimity, ended up moving us in with a man who I trusted would be *the* last one. In short, he was not, and on one hot sunny July day, this man cast us out of the house.

We were homeless.

Thankfully, one of my nieces welcomed us into her home until we found a place to live, which we did quickly, but not before another family member gave my niece tremendous grief about temporarily housing us, and also declared to me, "How dare you impose on her!"

Since then, my children and I lived on our own, although I did date someone until my story became a public one. At that point, I accepted my need to invest time in healing outside any romantic relationship, especially since my children had learned something of what happened to me in high school through an evening news sound bite version of the story. I realized that to have a good relationship with anyone else, I must first have a good relationship with myself. I must have a good relationship with myself first and foremost.

I had taken the first very small step toward more meaningful healing of my inner self.

CHAPTER SIX:

Healing Begins in Earnest

I will begin this pivotal chapter with a message from Spirit that graced me at precisely the right time and encouraged me to lean into my inner healing with earnestness. This message is presented just as I received it, and the narrative is somewhat peculiar in that I am referred to using the third person pronoun "she." No matter the third person perspective, though, the import of the message was and is profound, pointing the way for a transformation of my life and all the blessings that transformation eventually brings.

• • •

"For what is life but a passing of space between times that are not linear by true nature? As this mortal reflects upon times gone in her human existence, there have been many lessons and obstacles placed in front of her being in order to master whom she came here to be. In this mastery, life has not been kind in human terms, but yet she finds joy in her simple common life of everyday survival in her society. As she evolves, there is more of a divine essence that springs through her soul, connected to her beliefs, goals, and aspirations. She has faltered much in this lifetime, but has always followed her heart when the chips were down and there was nowhere to run, as if painted in a corner. Through her faith, often her blind faith, she has overcome some trials that sought to completely break her spirit and fracture her soul. This is what the sexual abuse by the priest, the unholy man of God, attempted to do within his unrighteous path of self-service to his body. She has risen from deep traumas that she has not yet ventured to visit inside her psyche, because she knows that some things are needed to be known to heal, while other things are better left unknown to her mind and clarified and cleared on the spiritual level instead."

• • •

In order to move forward with a higher level of healing, undertaking recovery of my inner self, I needed to carefully examine the years of my life before age 13, before Thomas Skotek's reassignment to St. Casimir's. I needed to do this self-assessment for three excellent reasons: to reconnect with my freer spirit from my pre-teen years, to search for any clues that might help me understand why Skotek had singled me out, and to honestly ask myself if anything I'd done had set me up as his mark.

Perhaps I could not have changed his actions no matter what, given that Skotek had my parents' blessings along the way, but it was still important that I ponder the "why me?" aspects of his targeting. I wished I could have been the proverbial fly on the wall on the day Skotek sought and gained my parent's permission for me to be a money counter at the rectory. Mom probably poured her heart out to him in lamentation about her wild child who'd already had sex with 16-year-old Wendel. Mind you, that had only happened once, and I carried much regret and shame about it in my own heart, but as I pondered all of this anew, an important question seemed to be what had led me to the one-time encounter with Wendel in the first place.

I scoured my memory repeatedly for clues from my relationship with my parents to relationships with my siblings; from a childish first kiss to early sensual experimentation; from secretive playtime fantasy to welcome or unwelcome advances; from being ogled on my way home from school to whatever else might have shown up on the conniving priest's perverse but perceptive radar. Of course, I have already mentioned the likelihood my parents told Skotek that I'd had sex once with Wendel, but I wanted to review and consider whether there was anything else the priest could have learned, sensed, or suspected that encouraged him to set his sights on me.

I will now forthrightly mention all the possibilities I could recall and leave it to the reader to guess if/how they factored in. For my part, I could not sort it out ultimately, because I was unable to fathom what might have gone on inside the twisted mind of that serial child molestor priest, or in the minds of other such offenders. Suffice it to say that I reviewed and considered all the things below, and then I accepted the fruitlessness of trying to definitively answer what for me proved to be the unanswerable.

I had extremely limited memories from my youth, and though I had no direct memories of my short-lived sister Stephanie, her brief life indirectly loomed large in my youth. I do remember my mother being in the hospital when Stephanie was born, and I recall not being allowed to go inside to visit, so I'd stood outside the hospital and waved up to Mom. But I don't remember the arrival of Stephanie into our home or her departure from this world so soon thereafter. I had her baby photo that was taken at the hospital, and I'd gaze at it in hopes that a memory would bleed through, and yet none did. However, I have clear memories of my mother in deep grief over the loss of Stephanie, of Mom locking herself in the basement to mourn while I stood at the locked door above. From that point on, Mom had far less to give, so I did not have a mother in the way all of my siblings had.

And speaking of my siblings, they were so much older than me — with the oldest 15 years my elder — that they had their own adult lives to live, and although they took me along to places here and there, for the most part I was alone. They were dating, getting married, and having children of their own by the time I reached the age of 10. So, I was a young girl who had so many changes and losses before age 12, and perhaps I was grieving the entire time with that grief manifesting as anger, rebellion, and too great a longing for love everywhere but from within. In retrospect, my mother was present yet absent. My father worked and worked some more. I spent countless hours listening to music, watching black and white television re-runs, and playing with my Barbie dolls. I did have a best friend, Ruth, during this time, but our friendship was lost when my family moved from town and then the priest entered the scene.

Noting that I was an attractive, blonde-haired and blue-eyed girl with a perpetual smile, many adults predicted aloud that I would be a heartbreaker. I would sing myself happy with songs such as "Open Up Your Heart and Let the Sun Shine In." I was probably more mature for my age than others, and I waxed vivacious, spunky, wanting to do, do, do. I was inquisitive, attentive, and alert to my surroundings. I was the one who would carefully listen to others and provide guidance, even as a youngster. I imparted wisdom for others, both then and later, even when my own life ironically became a tangled mess.

So, perhaps people were drawn to my energy, to my looks and light. Even in adversity, I appeared buoyant on the surface, despite my being, down deeper, a needy seeker of attention from others. I yearned for others to like me, to spend time with me, and my longing for someone, anyone, to give me attention may have sent out a beacon that attracted both good-natured people and selfish connivers like moths to a candle.

I also asked myself if I had been precocious and/or needy in terms of intimacy, and if so, what role(s) might that have played. The earliest memory I could bring up in this regard involved a party my siblings held in our family home, a party that included many of their friends when I was 5 or 6 years of age. I remember that one of their friends lay on a couch as the party progressed, and that I went over and hugged him. I then leaned across to kiss him on the lips, and he became all flustered, telling me get away or he'd tell my father. He did tell my younger brother, who was his friend, and I felt confusion and shame even though I have no recollection of being scolded about the incident. My sisters and brothers remained friends with that fellow through the years, but he and I always maintained our distance from that point on.

At age eight or nine, I often visited the home of my friend Martha, who lived in a duplex that included another family with a son named Davey. Martha and Davey frequently played together, and one day I joined them in the shared attic of their house, an attic set up with a child's kitchen, etc. We began to play house together, but then the two of them started kissing, which made me uncomfortable during the rest of the visit. But on a subsequent play day with Martha visiting me at my house, at one point, the two of us stretched out on the floor alongside my bed where we thought no one was able to see us. There, she and I by turns lay atop each other, kissing and touching. I cannot remember if we had our clothes on or not, but Mom discovered us, and thereafter she forbade me to visit Martha. This would have been a great opportunity for dialogue between Mom and me, but she initiated no discussion about the situation, and more shame took hold of my being.

I've mentioned playing with my Barbie dolls as a child, and I probably did so more often than is typical due to my degree of solitude, but what I did not mention until now is that I'd fantasize Ken and Barbie sharing intimacy. I would arrange the dolls' limbs and set up scenes to enact that fantasy, but I have no idea when or how I learned about what is euphemistically referred to as "the birds and the bees." My playtime imaginings may be altogether typical among children with anatomically correct dolls, or it could be that both my sexual awareness and curiosity were greater than was typical.

When I was still pre-teen, my breasts blossomed and the boys at school were keen on them. One day I was with some male classmate friends behind the school, and though I can't remember how or why we came to be there, I do remember there being three of them. They wanted to touch my breasts, and they did so even though I said no, and though I expressed my annoyance clearly. I never told anyone about the incident, but thereafter, I stayed clear of those boys and hated what they'd done.

I was not safe among my family unit, either, regarding untoward sexual advances. Various male family members who were connected by marriage made passes of some sort. One attempted to kiss me while he was intoxicated. Another made at least two attempts to hold my hand, and he also tried to touch my breasts while driving me in a car.

A third male relative was downright brazen. The setting was that he, his wife (my sister), and I were on a trip to Boston where they were to make an Amway business presentation. At the hotel room, while my sister was taking a shower, her husband reached out and drew me up to him, but I pulled away in disgust, demanded that he stop grabbing at me, and said I was going to tell my sister what he'd done. He promised to stop, to never do it again, if I would keep quiet, so I agreed and did not tell her until years later when other life events revealed several longstanding secrets.

When my family still lived in the town of Freeland, I would walk to school by myself or with some friends. Over a period of days during that time, some creepy old man followed me to and fro, and I remember him peering through the windows of our family's Laundromat at me from the side of the building. I brought this to Mom's attention after a day or two (thank God I at least spoke up about this!), and I later learned that the police arrested the man after Mom called to report the stalking.

So, when all of this was fresh in memory, I asked myself what the boys/man/priest thought they saw in me to dare these things, or whether that even had anything to do with it. Did I effectively have a big mark on my forehead that read: *Target!* due to my having been curious about sensuality with a few moments of experimentation? Or would they have fondled, grabbed, and stalked any girl, anywhere, anytime if they figured to get away with it? I do not know.

Having come to terms with my early childhood, and having accepted the unanswerable nature of many questions around it, I then needed to deal with issues of blame at my parents for subjecting me to Skotek's abuses. It may come as a shock to the reader, but by degrees, I came to no longer blame either parent for the priest's preying upon me or for the many subsequent breakdowns of our family ties. Both Mom and Pop were so devoted to the church and so mesmerized by Skotek's perfidious charisma that they were literally unable to break his spell. Priests were exalted at that time. They were put on a pedestal and could do no wrong. Therefore, it was considered a noteworthy honor for a family to have a priest in the house for dinner. My family solidly felt that I was safe with the priest, an honorable servant of the church, who abstained from sex. Having said this, I do believe that my father knew the truth to some small nagging degree within his heart – but he successfully kept it compartmentalized out of conscious awareness. Perhaps he subconsciously believed I had been a willing participant or even that I had initiated the sex. What I do know is that when the truth came out about what Skotek had done to me, my father laid the responsibility for it squarely at my feet. He declared that I "did something" to make it happen.

Mom had been mortified and full of remorse, so apologetic and trying to make amends for my pain, until the day she died. But Pop never apologized. In fact, the subject was never spoken about nor addressed by either of us after his initial assignment of fault to me. He took this to his grave, and I can say that I have only managed to fully forgive my father now. Over the years, he came through indirectly in spirit during classes that I took for psychic development, and I often became annoyed by his haunting appearances, again and again. Perhaps it was his way of expressing regret, but I was less than receptive.

Ultimately, however, I was gifted an apology in a most unexpected manner. The apology came via an Australian, a healer named Simon Hay, that my daughter went to when she was enrolled in school in the Land Down Under. Simon told my daughter that Pop was present there and that he wished for her to tell me how deeply sorry he felt. The words that I had so longed for were finally given to me, and it was so blessed a healing that, as I write this, tears tumble down my face in release and gratitude. I do at last forgive him, because even after death, he is trying to make amends for that wrong.

So, as I said, the sexual abuse broke down our family in any number of ways. Some in the family signaled they would wait for me to reach out to them, and sometimes I did; yet I endured this trauma for so long that my reaching out itself became incredibly difficult. I, at one time, blamed Skotek for my family's dismantling; later, though, I realized our own perceptions are what cripple our relationships. We all possess free will to rise above and move forward. Some rise above and move toward healing. Some hold the pain and grief inside only to have it morph into hatred or illness. While I worked toward understanding, I could remain locked in loss of family and grieve the loss of family togetherness at holidays and other times, or I could allow each family member to be himself or herself and accept how they chose to feel. I need not agree with anyone; I need to just acknowledge where they are and keep moving forward myself. Staying stuck in a cycle was not a good option for me, and it never has been. I always say to those having a difficult time that it is all right to be where you are, but don't stay there too long. The "too long" turns into shadows in the mind, body, and spirit that may take far longer still to dispel. There were times when I grew melancholy about the loss of blood family. There were times that I wished my children could have their extended family around, but then I realized that we each make choices in life. Mine was to heal myself and to raise my children in a home full of love, and the sections that follow will outline how I have manifested substantial healing, one small step at a time, and painfully often, with steps taken backward.

Early in my healing phase, I was forced by personal circumstances to ask two hard questions and to answer myself with brutal honesty. Honesty: Is a broken person deserving of a healthy relationship? Is a broken person deserving of beautiful and wonderful things?

I initially responded with a definite yes, but from the core of my being, I already knew it not to be true. Under the sway of that definite yes, I'd gotten involved with a broken man, even though I knew inwardly he was not healthy for me in numerous ways. I had rationalized that he and I were good for each other because we were both broken, perhaps for different reasons, but broken by life events, nonetheless. This, in my definite yes mind, created an unrealistic bond between us; I would fix him, and he would accept my damaged parts and me.

Well, I lost myself in that live-in relationship, almost totally. During most of our time together, his brokenness reared its head via insecurity and distrust toward me, with him always asking me where I was going and with whom, wondering why I did my hair a certain way, wore certain clothes, or put on makeup when going somewhere with my children. In an attempt to keep one step ahead of these glaring insecurities, I stopped wearing makeup, or dressing to look nice, or having friends visit. I cooked meals especially to suit him, I ventured places with him that he favored, I listened to him attentively whenever he wished, and I supported him in developing a stronger relationship with his children, yet none of this seemed to help him feel any more secure.

His insecurities were not only a reflection of his unhealed parts, but were also a mirror as to what he was doing when we were not together. After the relationship dissolved, I learned that he had been seeing other women during his and my time living together, but he blamed me for everything wrong about our relationship. I decided then and there that I would not accept anything less than exceptional in my next relationship.

I had loved that man with extra devotion, because having realized that I had not given my all in my previous relationships, I had resolved to give him my absolute best and make it work. Ultimately, I failed, neither due to a lack of trying nor lack of love but because two brokens do not make one complete whole.

I mourned the loss of him, and he moved on within two months. I, too, moved on, but the process of moving on was different for me that time around. I allowed myself time to grieve the loss of my expectations and my dreams. I grieved the loss of my time when I'd sunk and retreated into a basic daily grind. I grieved in many ways, and I will share some detail about these ways, because they have worked for me in healing throughout the years, particularly well in this situation.

Songs have the power to heal. I would hear certain songs and I would weep, but in that grief, I would play the same song repeatedly until the anger, sadness, loss left my body via tears, sobs, and breath. I would sing through the songs – well, I would attempt to sing through songs that stirred deep wounds. Then I would push repeat and push it again, as many times as necessary until the tears stopped flowing and my voice regained strength. This happened often, for I was frequently in the car driving. Today, I can listen to the same songs, but they feel quite different, because the grief that I had felt escaped with the healing. This has also been a self-regulation gauge in my healing. Because songs do trigger memories so effectively, I have avoided many of the songs from my teenage years. Some songs are regulators that help determine what yet needs to be reassessed and released, and some I can listen to in quiet reminiscence.

Another of my helpful healing techniques involved facing and accepting the reality that my lover had moved on. For a time, I would drive past the house that he still occupied with his new girlfriend, but by no means to stalk them, rather to force my recognizing that it was over so that I could and would move on. This approach to healing was not easy, but it certainly did succeed. The day that both of their vehicles were in the driveway was a day of great grief release. I cried for being replaced so quickly. I cried over the love that I felt for him. I cried over the love that was lost. The grief during those times was palpable, but each time that I drove by en route to a destination, albeit off the beaten track, the pain lessened, and the heartache subsided. To aid in my healing while not holding onto remorse, anger, pain that was beginning to be felt about his relationship, I genuinely sent them both love. I visualized them holding hands and walking away from me, but with a huge heart over them or on their hands with the intent that they had each other to love. This helped re-frame my thoughts toward him and them and substantially helped me move forward in my life.

Perhaps you are wondering why I would choose to send them love. When you genuinely love someone, you don't abruptly stop loving him or her. When you love them, you want them to feel love, feel peace, feel happiness. In this case, even though it wasn't with me, I still wanted the same for him (love, peace, happiness), so I sent them both unconditional love. The lessons that I have taken away from that relationship were necessary for my self-growth, and I thank him for the love he was able to give and the freedom he abruptly gave to me (us). It launched me to a greater understanding of self, who I was, who I wanted to become, and what I would and would not accept. I am grateful.

With focused resolve, I made a silent vow that I would fix whatever was broken in me, and I invested years in doing so and transformed into a different, more whole human. And that, in turn, allowed me to eventually take a new step: to live daily in such a way as to create the life that I do want. To arrive at this place of affirmative action, though, I first had to undergo years upon years of work fixing the broken aspects of me via cognitive therapy, psychoanalytical evaluation, Reiki, Eye Movement Desensitization and Reprocessing (EMDR), and Neuro-Linguistic Programming (NLP), with many of these merely scratching the surface of my counterproductive and deeply embedded beliefs, patterns, programs, and feelings. I hasten to add that all of these modalities contributed significantly to my healing process; to my knowledge, there is no one way to heal, no single means of healing.

At one point in my counseling/therapy, however, I began questioning the effectiveness of the whole therapeutic process. After all, I had then been in therapy at that point for more than 20 years. *When will this cycle stop? When will I no longer feel the need for therapy? Why isn't it helping like I want it to?*

I asked my therapist, who has been a lifeline, a godsend toward true healing, those questions, and she answered me in roundabout ways with suggestions for research on yet other metaphysical approaches to healing. She never came out and said,

"Audrey, you should do x, y or z," but instead provided me with life stories from her experiences that were relevant to mine. That is, she wisely handed me a set of door keys and let me choose which doors to unlock and which to leave unopened.

One particular key that she included was that of shamanic practices. I decided to open that door and peek in, and after my first glance, decided to swing the door wide open and stride in. It was, without a doubt, a shift that was needed. After much reading, listening, and learning about the history of shamanism and the beliefs behind it, I felt it was exactly what I needed next in my recovery. In shamanic practice, the belief is that during a traumatic event such as a car accident, sexual abuse, violence, or giving birth, the soul essence leaves the body in order to remove itself from the pains of the event. The soul essence does return to the body in most instances, yet sometimes it does not, and it can fragment instead. Thereafter, the soul fragments linger in a time and place away from the rest of the soul.

It is believed that such soul loss creates breaks in one's luminous field and draws to it life situations akin to the initial trauma. The symptoms of soul loss may include addictions, depression, post-traumatic stress, codependency, narcissism, low self-esteem, and adjustment disorders. Shamanic healing involves a shaman journeying on your behalf to retrieve soul fragments from different realms/planes of existence and reconnecting them to your soul essence. Powerful stuff, and this is what I felt that I might need.

I did.

My first experience of such healing was with Navajo medicine man, Sam Tso. I had no idea what to expect, but I was more than ready to break with the processes that ran loops in the background and stalled my healing progress.

That session with medicine man Tso was deeply healing, and for three days afterward, I experienced a succession of positive removals, clearings, visions from the work assignments the medicine man gave me. During the three-day period, I was not to touch, hold, or hug anyone, which was a big challenge for me, but quite eye-opening. Professionally, I was an early intervention speech therapist with youngsters in my care 3 to 5 years of age, and I had regularly held their hands while walking down the hall, or given a high-five or fist pump for a job well done, or even shared a side hug when they approached me. Before this shamanic exercise, I did not grasp how much of my personal energy I was extending or that others were receiving, but after the exercise, I felt a powerful shift. I had a greater strength and a greater sense of calm. And it was not that handholding or hugging was undesirable, per se; it was that I needed to be conscious of the dynamics involved and act accordingly.

My next experience involved a group setting led by Alberto Vivaldo and Marcela Lobos on an October weekend at Omega Institute. It was during their Rite of the Womb ceremony that I felt myself freed from fear and pain in my own womb, and I embraced the roles known as Earth Keeper and Womb Keeper.

My third experience with a shaman involved the soul retrievals I mentioned earlier and were with a Reiki-trained female shaman who had studied under Sandra Ingerman. This session was profoundly healing to my soul, and while not all of my soul fragments were ready to be returned home, many of them were integrated back into my being, and the renewing process continued later during a fourth shamanic experience with another shaman.

I continue to move forwards with healing and integration as my journey continue. Thankfully, at the time of this writing, I re-intergrate and re-establish more of my true soul self into this human meat suit I call home. I seek to regain the remaining parts of me that are merely lost and haven't managed to find the way home as yet, as opposed to my previous desperation to salvage an altogether broken spirit. For this, I am grateful. As my journey continues with the path of shamanic healing, I am now able to bring home soul parts that were in the ethers during journey sessions I do on my own. Also, I've found that I can integrate those restored parts by holding my own homecoming ceremonies, including such simple joys that were once elusive to me as eating grape licorice or having a bike ride in honor of reclaimed soul part.

In addition to the precious shamanic sessions, breath work also played a major role in my healing. Initially, I found that I would often not be breathing properly; perhaps with overlong pauses between breaths with or unconsciously holding my breath, but either of them in response to stress, anxiety, and life events playing out. Fortunately, I discovered that area of self-improvement and attended multiple breath work events that provided me with valuable healing techniques, albeit each different in intensity and content. Each of these techniques helped me suspend racing thoughts and emotions while opening me up both to messages from spirit and to pivotal revelations.

I feel the need to add here that one cannot merely march through the steps of the healing process perfunctorily. It's necessary to approach any of the modalities by first setting one's intentions with clarity and purpose, as opposed to just checking off some list of meditations, assignments, or exercises. At the times that I felt a lack of clarity, I learned to allow my higher self to step in and guide the process, and that always lead to me receiving whatever was necessary. By trusting in the process and letting Source flow freely, by stepping out of the fears of what could possibly go wrong and embracing the possibilities of everything that could go right, much greater healing occurred.

In addition to the shamanic practice and breath work, I also became interested in an approach called Theta® healing. In the first evening group session I attended, there were four offerings: Healing Trauma/Soul Retrieval, DNA Activation, Loving Yourself, and Connecting Back to Source. And though my relationship with my higher power had been shaky in adulthood, I thought that I had recovered it rather well, but for some fortunate reason, I chose the fourth option named Connecting Back to Source, nonetheless. During this powerful session, as I sat quietly with the practitioner's hand upon my shoulder, I felt tears well up then start freely running down my face, and thought to myself *What a big baby I am! This is ridiculous!* But afterwards, I reached up to swipe at the plentiful tears still on my face, and to my supreme astonishment, there were none there! My face was dry, and not one physical tear had fallen. On the other hand, ample spiritual tears had fallen from my higher self, yes, and I had felt them roll down ethereally. The session leader pointed out that, despite resistance by me, I had indeed reconnected to Source more directly.

I was in awe. I returned home to consider what I had experienced, and some nights later, dreamt that I was walking upon a ledge and someone shoved me off it. As I fell, plunging down fast, I heard myself screaming that I did not jump, but that I was pushed. At that moment, a bright square appeared, one that transformed into a rectangle and safely landed me on the ground where I calmly strode through a forest. I had indeed been pushed, and Spirit saw this, assisting me to land rooted in the Earth's soil and able to wend my way through the woods. I was back to God, Creator of all that is, and I felt it deeply.

Much has changed from that time. I took a class on writing master prayers, again strengthening my bond with my higher power, and I went on to become a Theta® practitioner (DNA I and DNA II) and using this healing work was able to propel myself forward in my soul purpose. In due time, I no longer considered my progress toward greater understanding of myself as "work," since the word work has some negative connotations for our society; instead, I considered it movement toward something greater. All that I formerly regarded as hardships and traumas I came to think of more as steppingstones.

Sometimes I faltered in these beliefs, of course, for I am human, but that became increasingly acceptable as I grew.

Someone could easily look upon my words as crazy and out of touch with society, or even out of touch with myself, because I choose not to wallow in grief, anger, hostility, bitterness, or subjugation for long periods of time, if at all. And I freely admit that for me to have any sense of normalness or sanity throughout my youth, I did need to bury memories for a time. But later, I recognized it is best that I acknowledge them, let them rise like molten lava that has been dormant, let them bubble, spew over, and then cool in a new form, freed and renewed in the complete and total power of my being. And this is just what I did by way of the various modalities already mentioned, and during the more recent experience of a plant medicine journey. I allowed everything to bubble up and spew out in coughs and waves of release of that which had marred my being for far too long. I had listened once again to my own inner knowing as to what was needed on my personal journey and I it finally showed the deep freedom I so long searched and strove for. I became free to be me.

Whatever modality might be called upon at a given time, it is particularly useful to revisit past relationships and to assess emotions, hurts, or beliefs from those relationships in a new light. For example, I often use people who enter back into my life as personal gauges for how my growth is proceeding, which proves doubly valuable, because it allows me to re-assess feelings of then versus now. How does my body feel around them? If I allow this person to touch my hand, what internal response do I have? If I allow this person to speak face-to-face with me, how does my body react? Is there tension in my body anywhere and if there is, why? Is it a present feeling within my body or something that can and should be released from my cell memory?

I met with a man from my past recently — the one who had summarily put me and the children out of his house on a hot July day — and upon his request, allowed him to touch my hand then to hold it for the duration of our time chatting. I allowed this because I felt honesty in his voice, sincerity in the words he spoke. I knew that he was reaching out forthrightly to ask for forgiveness, to make amends, and to heal what had been deeply fractured between us. He said to me that he now realizes what hell he put me through and the wrongs he brought about when we were together. He said that he had had a great woman and had lost her.

All of this was unexpected, but nothing is ever random in our Creator's eyes, is it? Perhaps those moments were closure he needed with me. Perhaps they were closure I needed with him. Perhaps both. I do know that I am not the same woman he sent packing years ago. I am stronger and wiser, forgiving, but clearer. I remember the life that I tried to create with him for all of us, for him, for his and my children, and for myself. I am grateful for his trust in me along his journey, and since that time of healing, I am glad to say he has possibly found his soul partner.

I think that in the past, both he and I were classic examples of a syndrome common in our society today: afraid to be happy. Yes, for much of my life, I held the debilitating notion that happiness was too risky. Put another way, I believed that if I embraced happiness, something sad would overwhelm it as a matter of certainty. If I became remarkably happy, something remarkably bad would by definition supplant it. So, I dread the very concept of happy. I dwelt in fear of happy, and all things happy. I allowed happy to elude me, and I eluded happy, staying away from it as though it were a vampire. Perhaps that constant fear of happy stemmed from my trauma, from my victim mentality. It was as if

I believed, *Oh, my God, if I appear to be happy, then they will think that all is well in my world!*

So, here is the thing: I fought away happy much of my life, and after years upon years of shadow work, deep soul searching, and healing inner and outer wounds, I'll be darned if I haven't found my happy. And I rejoice in my heart finally finding more pieces and coming together as a healthy unit. Finding that happy has been quite a process but a worthwhile one.

How about an example of me being locked away from happiness, but then working to restore it in my life to great joy? After I'd started college and therapy, my trips to the New Jersey beaches essentially stopped. My great love of the sand and water was washed away by painful memories, at least until I became stronger again. It was not until my oldest daughter was born that I returned to the beach at Cape May, New Jersey again, after more than 10 years of staying away from a place that I felt alive and free. I remember having flashbacks of times on the beaches of New Jersey during those early return visits, and they were painfully difficult, but I had two new reasons to continue and move through those memories: my daughter, and claiming my own happy. I can now go to the New Jersey beaches with little or no issues. What once was heighted awareness as to which beaches I needed to avoid and which I could enjoy has now ended. I am now free to enjoy the energies of the sand and surf. I value life. I value all life.

There were so many modalities that played a part in my healing process and overcoming my fear of happy, and some key concepts among those modalities include acceptance, forgiveness, love, and being in the present moment.

But, as I have mentioned a number of times, healing for most others and me rarely takes place in anything resembling a straight line. In fact it is most often a case of two steps forward and one back, or it can even be a case of one step forward and two (or three) back! Therefore, the fractures of my spirit caused me to revisit occurrences repeatedly in an onion-peel-spiral type of way; I often became frustrated with the idea that my healing was so much like trying to peel an onion, as it was seemingly never-ending and typically led to tears at each, next attempt.

So, the healing was and is sometimes slow, sometimes inconsistent, and yet the healing goes on. From the outside looking in, it may appear that I have been a hot mess of uncertainty to some, and this may have often been the case. The healing approached I undertook led to an unraveling of old beliefs and old steadfast patterns that formerly enabled me to survive, but then stood in my way. I see how examining those beliefs and patterns alternately closed my heart hard and opened it, oh, so slowly.

Thankfully, a distant Reiki master and friend cautioned me about closing off my heart to love after I had experienced a particularly deep heartache and breakup. On his advice, I did not close off my heart to myself, but rather took the time to contemplate the profound truth of something I'd been told through the years: first, I needed to love myself. I remember having gotten quite upset with people telling me this in the past, because I thought that I already loved myself, so what was the fuss about with these people needlessly revisiting the topic? After all, I reasoned, it mattered not what type of love I had found, whether it was a mutual love or a love based on physical needs or a love based on the mentality that I had at the time.

Previously, I had simply failed to grasp what loving myself entailed. When I finally gave the concept its due, the whole thing made sense, and I opened up to the wisdom of it, but it's been an ongoing and often awkward process of trial and error, nonetheless. What I found quite important in my personal journey toward loving myself included time to just be attuned to myself and with myself without outside influences. I very much needed to decide what I needed to have in my life, in honor of myself. This, for me, meant taking the time to sit and just be alone at various times of day. It also meant for me to practice meditation on a weekly basis and to develop inner gifts that lay dormant.

I remember first attending a group meditation on a Friday night by myself, not already knowing anyone else present, but knowing that I was welcomed just the same. In subsequent group meditations, I would release the burdens from my week and, to a degree, from my entire life. I remember thinking and saying aloud that I hoped one day I could get through a meditation without need for tissues and tears. The tears were often those of release, release of what might have been or could have been, or release of broken expectations finally being liberated from deep inside me. The tears were of healing the present and releasing the past, which tried to hang on desperately, knowing that a new path, a new and better way of life, was coming. Those group meditation nights were freeing to me in many ways and led to seasons of deeply profound healing that I could only do for myself, but with the supportive guidance of my spiritual team here on earth and in the heavens.

In finding myself through these meditations, I realized that what I once deemed love had amounted to unhealthy attachments fueled by codependency, but that was one hard-won realization. I fought long and stubbornly against accepting the term "codependency" as applying to my behavior, because I wanted to depend upon no one except me, or at least that was my limiting belief and opinion that I had set myself up to believe. I still realize today, even up to and including the moments of writing this chapter, that I remain too fiercely independent for my own sake, and I need to learn better the art of trusting and allowance of outreached hands of support.

In time, a truth could no longer be denied: healthy relationships were foreign to me. I had pictures in my mind about relationships and how they should look, mostly from my family, acquaintances, and media. My three marriages speak volumes to this healing evolution I underwent. My first husband, Pete, was one of the kindest, most loving and honest men that I have ever met, and he loved me at my absolute worst. We met when I was not yet healed from the emotional, physical, nor mental trauma of the clerical abuse, and I was consequently unstable, insecure, and neurotic. I was in hospital for depression while with him. I was also taking nascent steps toward getting to know myself, but unfortunately for this compassionate man, I was simultaneously and prematurely grasping for love outside myself.

Pete loved me. He sincerely loved me, as did his family, and I was blessed with their kindness and understanding, both during our relationship and afterwards, with the tragedy being that I was not developed enough to adequately receive and reciprocate that love, kindness, and understanding. Had I done my own inner work beforehand, that marriage would likely have flourished.

As it did play out, though, Pete's sister introduced me to the healing modality known as Reiki, and that connection initiated an acceleration of my healing. Reiki is described as an energetic medicine that works on balancing the body, mind, and spirit. It is a modality that helps remove stagnant energy (trapped emotions) from the body's energetic system. The female Usui Reiki master, Lorraine, that I was honored to train with also incorporated other healing modalities to help me remove what no longer served me. Those additional modalities included past life regression, intuitive guidance, and Neuro-Linguistic Programming, the last of which is often abbreviated NLP. She represented an important lifeline, healing my wounds and providing me hope to move forward in my life. Our connection spanned years with her not only providing healing, but with her sharing and teaching me the wisdom and ways of healing. She trained me to become a Reiki master/ teacher even as she helped me learn to master myself, and from these grand experiences, my passion for true healing still stands decades later, and I employ the variety of modalities mentioned in previous pages to remove traumas from my psyche, my body, my spirit. I've never stopped learning or refining my beliefs concerning the life I once lived, and I look compassionately at others who sit in pain, anger, and hostility, for I recall the long years throughout which I did this myself. Those earlier years involved so much internal combustion it is a wonder I survived to speak of them.

The Neuro-Linguistic Programming I mentioned above specifically helped me deal with undesirable triggers, which refers to anything that set off counterproductive reactions in me, and of which there were a great number. By me learning to identify both conscious and unconscious negative triggers, I could intone *Cancel, Cancel, Cancel!* with strong intention and nullify them. Each time I was triggered negatively, the intensity varied, but in time, the intensity dissipated. I had tremendous success with NLP done with my trained mentor, Lorraine. One means I learned of using NLP was to still my mind. It allowed me to envision being guided to a seat in an otherwise employ movie theatre, fully safe among the stillness of the other empty chairs and large screen. Then, I would begin watching reels of scenes from my own life, but when traumatic moments came onto the screen, the projector would be halted, the movie reel removed, and the disturbing scene literally edited out of the film, for it was no longer needed.

So, dear reader, my healing process for these pains is clearly multi-faceted — and perhaps beyond the realm of what some would think of as normal — but it certainly has worked for me, and I have also used this eclectic, creative approach to help me heal my sexual strife as well. For example, I had had considerable success in healing my heavy heart from romantic disillusionments through the Theta Healing Heart Song, so I was inspired to modify this heart song and use it for the purpose of activating my base chakra. That is, I rewrote the song to address my sexuality.

This process, too, was successful, although I realize that it may seem peculiar to others and embarrassing as well. But, I felt my sexual health depended upon it, especially given that the trauma of cell memory caused erogenous parts of my body to hurt with every move. The stabbing phantom pains in my vaginal walls and uterus needed to stop, and if they were to stop, I would see to it myself, perhaps with some knowledgeable guidance.

I have no name for my healing practice to move past the pains that are untestable and psychological in nature, but I declare that my practice was beneficial. No matter how uncomfortable I was with my body, particularly my complete vaginal structure, I knew that I wanted to be healthy in my sex life. I decided that the abuse was not going to stop me from experiencing the bliss that orgasm can bring a woman, even a woman who has been sexually assaulted, sexually abused, sexually degraded. So, I developed this technique and managed to rid myself of much pain. I also did healing work on my beliefs and feelings around sexual relations and intercourse. I am not a prude, nor am I a swinger. I am just a woman who wants to feel good within her own skin, within her own body. I want to feel sensual and be able to entice my divine soul life partner in positive ways that partners do.

I'll give a description of this self-styled sexual healing technique. Taking the same approach of the original Heart Song, which is going into a gentle meditative state, I'd start singing my revised version of the song, actually lamenting my vagina. As I sang, I'd touch the lips that had held onto the pain, the hurt, the guilt, the shame, my rape as a teen, and my lack of respect for my own body in my adult years. I recalled how I had felt, touching there and making vowel and consonant vocalizations that sounded like mournful orcas lamenting a lost member of the pod. I undertook these healing exercises in privacy, of course, so that I could complete them without interruption or anyone's embarrassment.

This technique was no quick fix that felt neither right the first nor even the second time, but I continued nonetheless, and as I continued, the lamentations and deep grief began to abate and release. I was able to lift my voice a bit higher, and with each healing session, my libido returned gradually. I learned to explore who I was sexually, what I liked sexually, and for the first time in my life, I finally felt free from the sexual abuse by having become intimate with myself. The biggest obstacle I faced was returning control of my body fully to myself, but by facing it, I found additional strength and a sense of pride that I did not falter in my healing process; I just advanced in a new and unique manner.

I will continue on the subject of sexual healing. Through the years, I have had many therapists, psychiatrists, counselors, and one psychologist pointed out there are two distinct outcomes from people who have experienced abuse: either they become frigid, or they become hypersexual. In my past, I was the latter. I do not dwell on the people that I was with. Some were just passing in time, some touched my heart and soul, and some meant nothing to me at all, and some still want me again. It was not until my third marriage of 12 years that I managed to be wholly faithful for a sustained period of time.

When it comes to sex for me now as I heal, I find that it is not about the act but about the meaning behind the passion of the act of making love. I am choosing now, as an adult, whom I allow into my womanly space. I choose to whom I open up my legs, as well as my heart. I have recently realized that, although I do know what makes me feel good during lovemaking, I am learning what I personally enjoy, and I am in process of learning how to express myself freely. I know how to please a man, for the most part, but I am not a confident lover. I do not know what to say or how to say it without feeling awkward but I am learning and evolving. Yes, I have been with many, but the focus was on pleasing that person. What do you want me to say? What position do you want to try? How do you like it? But when asked what I want, I freeze in uncertainty. I cannot believe that, as a mature woman, I do not know exactly what to say to a man to let him know what I like or want. It feels uncomfortable for me, and I draw a blank and as this book is in process, so is my ability to request what I want, need and desire.

So, what do I like? I like warm embraces, gentle kisses, soft touches. I like getting lost in making love and falling off the bed. I like stopping and talking. I like the cozy feeling of snuggling after making love. In the passion of sex, I vary, but I do like passion in general. I like crazy positions and unusual places.

As yet, I do not like dressing up and pretending to be someone else. I know where that dislike comes from and have been earnestly working through this block. I have done a boudoir studio photo shoot, just for myself, to move through the emotions that have limited me from loving my body as it is. It was a powerful move toward coming back into self-awareness of parts of myself that I had neglected much too long. Pampered care at a beauty salon, shopping for undergarments and clothing, or getting nails done were never in my norm of care. Who knows, perhaps some of these things I will manage to transfer to my "like" list in due time?

Overall, in a strange kind of way, I am a success story. I have overcome many years of self-doubt and self-loathing, but I have always persevered. I go on. That is what I do. And during the past few years, my views of sex have morphed from a bodily act between lovers into a spiritual act between two souls; a union made in awareness of spirit, a union made in awareness of soul. For me now, sexual relationship is sacred: a melding of two, providing sustenance and nurturing of heart that transcends time and space. This journey into my sexual healing and sexual awareness has not been an easy one for me, but it has been one that I am glad to have moved toward. There is sacredness within the sharing of breath, sharing of energy, sharing of conscious that transcends the negative experiences that I endured earlier in life.

Any full account of my healing journey must absolutely address the role of prescription medications, for I had many bouts of severe depression that counseling alone could not fix before I'd discovered and fully employed the many excellent healing modalities already mentioned. Medication turned out to be the answer for me back then, and to a lesser degree, for much of my adult life.

A psychiatrist that I was seeing early on prescribed lithium after diagnosing me with bipolar disorder. However, his recommended cocktail of Prozac and lithium was too much for my body, and I ended up in a psychiatric hospital for a week or two. I was treated and released, and then I continued with other medications, but not under the care of the doctor who had diagnosed me as bipolar disorder. It was later determined that I had severe depression and PTSD.

Through my counseling sessions with the new psychiatrist, I learned a valuable lesson, one that stayed with me through the years. The lesson? That one can never say *I don't know*, because deep down somewhere is the answer. It may be an answer that is not pleasant to acknowledge or hear, but it is still an answer.

I had one more visit to a psychiatric hospital, and that came about at Christmastime in the first year I was married. I had found our new life just too hard and complicated, and I needed a break, so I admitted myself and was there only for a week. Afterwards, I continued with cognitive therapy sessions, as well as medications off and on, throughout adulthood. However, when I became pregnant with my first daughter, I went off medications and did not use them again until a second marriage was falling apart. Years of psychiatric visits and countless cognitive therapy sessions have been almost a mainstay in my life, peppered with shorter periods when I was drug free and not seeing a therapist.

I should like to conclude this chapter on my long road toward healing with three current affirmations that reveal my sense of determination, hope, and joy, and I trust that you will find in them something that speaks to your own wholeness and health. I begin with a favorite that has to do with conscious breathing.

- It is now that I speak from my heart space and find that judgment is softened through this route. I do this by closing my eyes, taking a few long breaths in through my nose, breathing in light/love, and exhaling scattered thoughts or unkind words. I visualize love entering my heart with each inhalation, and anything not of love leaving. This helps center me. I bring the energy in, and as I speak from my heart, I see words of kindness and love exiting my mouth via words. Keep doing it. It is a process in process, yet it is an attempt to go within and still the random ramblings of a programmed belief that no longer serves my highest good.

- I rise in triumph over my past and the illusion of any pain is gone. I stand upright in knowing that my life has unfolded as my soul has planned. Make no mistake: pain, distrust, and even anger linger, but as they rise and surface, I adjust, release, and rest. It is after the rest that I can move on.

- I shift old beliefs and patterns and in doing so, I evolve back into a more loving being. I will sing the tones of my heart in order to freely and honestly love again. I break down my heart wall and welcome in love, giving and receiving with balance and flow. That is what I have done. My walls are coming down around my heart as I heal the beliefs and programs. My heart becomes open and alive with happiness and joy that had eluded me for too long. The illusion of a barrier between the heart and soul space has been dissolved and I am free to love. I am free and ready to love. As I step into self-love, I create space in me to love another.

CHAPTER SEVEN:

Grand Jury Report

Ah, but sometimes just when you think you finally have life by the horns, a tiger by the tail, and maybe even the world as your oyster, the most unexpected event can test you to new limits. Such was the case when, at age 51, I was broadsided, hit from out of the blue. Broadsided is not as much a reference to an automobile accident as it is to a shipwreck.

August 14, 2018 was a day like most other August days in Pennsylvania, warm and humid, with rain on the way. Work would start for me in a few weeks, and my children were getting things together for their new school year while enjoying the few remaining summer vacation days. It was my partner's birthday, and life was flowing along rather harmoniously.

On this fateful day, I was driving along an interstate high-way toward the city of Hazleton, near my hometown of Freeland, when my phone dinged to indicate a message had come through from my sister. Her text stated simply, "You made the newspaper today." I could sense undertones in her words, but I had no clue what she meant, so I phoned my birthday boyfriend and asked him if he could sort it out. He looked in the local newspaper and could find no mention of my name, only a story about the release of a Pennsylvania grand jury report on sexual abuse by Catholic clerics of our state, a report release that my boyfriend had previously mentioned to me as having been imminent. Well, I had had no striking reaction to my boyfriend's earlier remarks, and I didn't think the new newspaper coverage of the report release related to me, either, for I'd not been called in connection with that investigation nor had I been any part of the process. Obviously, I cared very much about the subject of calling out sexual abusers, but my struggles to expose and stop Skotek had taken place decades earlier, and as detailed in the previous chapter of this book, I'd invested much of the time since then getting healed and putting together a good life for myself.

In short, the report release did not concern me directly at all...until it did.

I asked my boyfriend to forward the report findings to my phone as I traveled, and I remember pulling to the side of the road on my way back home in order to read the material — not all of it, just the section concerning the Diocese of Scranton where Skotek had been harbored for so many years.

To my shock and dismay, I saw documents in that section with my date of birth, hometown, and name included!

My sister was correct; I certainly did make it into the paper. My ex-husband called, asking if I was all right. *No, I certainly am not. Who should I call? What should I do?* At his suggestion, I called the local congressman, but he was unavailable. Next, I called Tara Toohil, the state representative of the area where I'd grown up, and had to leave a message for her. She returned my call rapidly, and I — in a tumult of emotion — told her that my private story had been exposed in the news through attorney general Josh Shapiro.

Tara declared that she was on it. She would make calls and get back to me. In the interim, I too made frantic calls to the attorney general's office. *My name and my story have just been revealed to the entire world. I need to speak to someone right now!* I received no return calls until after Ms. Toohil was able to contact them. A person from the office of victim advocates finally called me to acknowledge that, indeed, my name had not been redacted.

Mortified. Numb. Grief-stricken. My children sensed something was terribly wrong. I wasn't ready to talk. I needed time to wrap my head around the events of the day.

I then went to my boyfriend's home, only to find that I was also featured on the television evening news. There upon the TV screen was my abuser Skotek and his accomplice Bishop Timlin being at last exposed publicly, but with my sensationalized life story as the focal point. My heart felt ripped open, I sobbed inconsolably on my boyfriend's shoulder, and that poor man had to deal with all of this on his birthday.

Without any notice, the media catapulted my life into the midst of this scandalous exposé, and then splashed it about liberally. My story was no longer the family secret. It was no longer secret at all. It was the opposite of a secret. It was broadcast.

My children learned more than I had hoped they ever would about that part of my life: that I had been sexually abused by my church priest for years, that I had had an abortion, that I had signed a non-disclosure agreement, and that I'd received money as a settlement. In a heartbeat, it had become necessary to share even more about this with my perplexed daughters and son, so I tearfully explained to them what had happened to me in a condensed version without the extent or complexity of it. I spoke to them about the option of saying and doing nothing versus stepping forward to tell my story in hopes that laws would get changed and other people would take up the cause. And I said to them that, if it seemed likely to help, I was willing to tell my story publicly.

Thankfully, both of my daughters and my son responded that they would support my decision, whatever it might be.

Thereafter, the only question any of my children put to me came from my eldest, Julianna, who wanted to know why I'd never told them before. I answered that I hadn't thought they needed to be burdened with such a dark shadow out of my past, but that I hoped the dark shadow would help explain my very protective approach to parenting.

The media coverage continued. Imagine my grief, distress, and horror when Skotek and Timlin's names were spoken in the same sentence about the girl who had the abortion…me. Imagine seeing it repeatedly on the television news. Imagine the judgments put upon me. Imagine seeing your story, your truth, on lawyer's websites in relation to clerical abuse.

And leading up to these shattering revelations, the Diocese of Scranton never provided so much as a hint to me that the agreement I'd signed with them had been shared with the attorney general's office. They never even told me that office was investigating them, and the attorney general never contacted me to let me know that they had my paperwork or that my truth was going to be told to the masses.

As if that were not enough to trigger me a hundred times over, I read in the grand jury report that Bishop Timlin had actually written letters of apology, letters of sympathy, to Skotek and other pedophiles!

How dare he! was my initial gut reaction, but then I remembered my phone calls and conversations with this supposed man of God, and I resigned myself to the fact that it was more of same.

Sigh!

The frequency and intensity of my reactions to this news cyclone did provide a fairly accurate barometer of my healing, though. Prior to the grand jury report being made public, I had been progressing well in an intimate relationship with the supportive boyfriend I mentioned several times above. I considered the man a possible life partner, and my overprotective shield had finally begun to disintegrate. He and I shared deep, intense intimacy of two souls connecting the matrix of our bodies. We intertwined our breaths and shared the gifts of our spirits. It was magical, mesmerizing, and holy. It was tantric passion, and I experienced love in a pure form. I had even allowed myself to become playful in the bedroom, and my lover had gotten through to me how beautiful I was by way of intimate photos I let him take of my derrière in sexy undies. This was a major step in healing for me, and I found it highly encouraging.

But then came the unexpected revelations in the media. I still tried to be intimate with my lover, but I had to halt lest memories might have flooded back and attached themselves to my time with him. And it further strained our intimacy when my libido quickly evaporated. I tried to recover and carry on, but I simply could not do so in the wake of the media storm.

Even at that, my man was patient and loving, providing me the space and safety I needed to heal in my own way. He shared with me a meditative technique called OM-ing that helped me release a lot of pain stemming from my former life. I was, and always will be, grateful to him, but as one might guess, I chose to walk away from this compassionate and understanding man. As I have indicated before, such is the aftermath from the sexual abuse I endured as a child, and likewise, such too was the fall-out from the television exposure in August of 2018 of my painful past abuse.

Two weeks of roller coaster emotions followed. Watching and checking to make sure my kids were all right. Making sure that the PTSD did not return full force, but fearing that it would. Staying away from the news, save for snips here and there. Moving forward. Moving back. Resting as best I could. Listening and thinking. Fielding calls, texts, conversations that engulfed my life following the report release.

Fast-forward to September 7, 2018, the day I drove down to the state capital and to the attorney general's office, the first and only official meeting that I would ever have at that office. School was now back in session, but I had been granted a conference day off work by my district superintendent, so I drove down to Hazleton then on to Harrisburg with state representative Toohil who had come to my rescue some three weeks earlier. I would be remiss if I did not add that my granted conference day was rescinded and made into a personal day with no notification made to me nor any reason given to me for the change.

Ms. Toohil and I met with the deputy attorney general and two representatives from the Office of Victim Advocate. Formalities were exchanged, and I was thanked for coming into the office, being told it was great to finally meet me. When I questioned the deputy attorney general about the office not having contacted me, he simply stated that they could not find me. He claimed that the state's investigators could not locate me, either, and that my name could not have been redacted, anyway, because the attorneys for the dioceses would then have countersued to redact all of the accused pedophile priests' names, too. The attorney general's office simply could not have gone that route, he said, because the Vatican had more legal counsel and money than did the state of Pennsylvania.

Therefore, he claimed, my name, hometown, and date of birth had to be included and could no longer be redacted.

The deputy attorney general went on to say their office was getting numerous calls from others that had undergone abortions at the demands of priests, nuns, and religious persons, implying that I should feel good that my story was helping others come forward to speak their truths.

After I excused myself to use the facilities and regroup, I returned to the meeting and to ask again, pointedly, why I had not been contacted, given that a simple Google search of my name immediately presented all of my married names, and a slightly deeper search turned up my address and phone number in an instant. Well, they just could not find me, I was told.

This was painfully reminiscent of my dealings with the District Attorney's office in Luzerne County when I was trying to expose Skotek's abuse of me. It was also painfully reminiscent of my dealings with Bishop Timlin when I was trying to prevent Skotek from abusing yet more children.

Sigh! And sigh, again!

I want to make it clear that I have always lived in the state of Pennsylvania and have never moved beyond a one-hour radius of the town in which I was born and raised. They could have found me easily. I know that, and they know that, but perhaps they didn't want to find me so they could sidestep the issue of redacting my name and, therefore, avoid the legal battle with the Vatican over redacting the priests' names as well.

In any case, they could have found me. Period.

From My Journal

In the aftermath of that media blitz and frustrating confer-ence, I calmed down enough to read the PA grand jury report, to contemplate the impacts of it on society at large and my personal life, and to realize that significant positive changes were likely on the horizon. Perhaps the Catholic Church would at last have to address the issue of child abuse forthrightly, perhaps society at large would move to protect children much better, and perhaps I would actually learn to rejoice in having been freed of those dark burdensome secrets, even though the secrets surfaced in such an unnerving manner.

It will soon be evident what path forward the Catholic Church and/or society at large choose, but as for me, I must admit feeling as though a millstone had been taken from around my neck, and I set about thinking, praying, and meditating on that blessing in the weeks, then months, following the disturbing upheavals. This new and deeper round of soul searching is evidenced in my journal entries below, the first of which was written less than two weeks after the disappointing meet up at the attorney general's office.

Even where the journal entries reveal a retreat of two steps back — or maybe three — I am pleased to see my eagerness in these passages to pause, regain balance, and again move forward.

Journal Entry of 9/20/2018

The deepest darkest secret of my life was revealed to all, and I guess it is time to unpack it. I am a murderer. I murdered my unborn child because I did not have the courage to run, run from a perverse man who forced his fear of being revealed upon me. Oh, hindsight, how my heart aches with what life has brought to me and how I have handled it! I am trying so hard to maintain a higher vibration, yet I struggle. I looked in the mirror this morning and I saw a tired woman, older with dark circles.

How might I make things better? For one thing, I can compel the Vatican to stand and work with legislators to repeal and change the laws. That would show an act of good faith toward healing for all survivors. The Vatican has the capability to move the church toward changes, the Vatican has the power to stand beside the survivors now and make radical changes, unprecedented in religious history. It will mean that they have to squirm, it will mean that they will need to pay out money to those survivors who had no voice within the legal system, but it would certainly signal they are serious about stopping the madness that has been occurring for so many years! Yes! Ask them to join the cause for reform of the laws. Go Big. Checkmate!

Journal Entry of 10/9/2018

How can I find beauty in the world today when laughter resides in the hearts of so few? How can I find laughter in the hearts of few when love dies hard on a concrete floor littered with broken dreams and tattered promises? How can I find beauty amongst the rubble of souls who have only a dim spark? How can I see the beauty in forgiveness when I have not yet fully forgiven myself, when I have not forgiven my family for failing to rescue me? How could I not have rescued myself from the flames that burnt all around me and engulfed my entire being — my entire life? I will not dwell in the land of the past for too long, for there is darkness and scary things that bite at my toes while I sleep. I will not continue the locked-in trigger patterns that impaled my progress toward freedom upon a quivering, jagged arrow shot from Hades. I am older and free, free to choose the paths that have the potential to send my soul into pure freedom, but at what cost? Is there a cost for freedom? And if there is a price for true freedom, which part of the body sells for the highest price?

Journal Entry of 10/14/2018

I fought with vigor for normalcy, until I realized that there is no real normal. Normal is a simple illusion created by beliefs that serve society rather than an individual. What was once abnormal and socially unacceptable has become the new normal in our society. Thousands upon thousands are now raped or otherwise abused daily in our world. What was once considered taboo and frowned upon now occurs within homes, within schools, within our religious systems, and our culture continues to allow the new norm to occur. How, as women, have we allowed our conscious-ness to accept the loss of our personal, spiritual power over our bodies? How have we, as women, allowed the new norm to be governed by the sexual drive of men rather than by the beauty of spiritual engagement and connection on a less beastly level?

Rape, defined by me, is a violent act done toward a male or female without their consent in abuse of body, mind, and spirit. Rape, by standard definition, is sexual activity carried out by force or under threat against a person's will or beneath a certain age.

How did I get from victim to survivor to warrior? It was a process. It was not a task that was easy, nor was it painless. It is easy to acknowledge the shadow side of self, but when one walks with the shadow side of self and experiences dark nights of the soul, great transformation often follows. You matter. Reach out. Hold space. These are all things that have brought me to tears in hope. I wish I believed in my heart of hearts that I do, indeed, matter and that my thoughts and feelings are not pure madness.

Journal Entry of 4/21/2019 – Easter Sunday

It has been quite a learning year for me, to say the least. I have learned whom my friends are and how easily people can leave your life, sometimes as they speak lies about others without bothering to open to the person(s) they berate or even begin to empathize. I have learned to value truth even more and to trust that it will always surface. I've learned, even more, how important and valuable my kids are in my life, and I had it pointed out to me this spring that I always seem to put them first, which is much to my liking.

I value those who have made me laugh this past year, who stopped by for a beverage on my porch just because they knew I was alone, or who graciously helped me calm my fears. Those loving souls will forever have a place in my heart. In these months I hit rock bottom, or so I thought, before I then fell further and deeper. But despite these struggles, I've re-developed a bit of the faith in God and Universe that I had foolishly discarded earlier in life, and I've come to be less concerned what other people think of me. I'm a different person than I was last April, much different, and I am pleased to note that life has changed me for the better this year.

This morning, I am wondering: Just what are the words *I love you* but a mantra repeated time and time again? In a relationship, so many feelings whirl around those three simple, yet powerful words. Where do these words fit into your relationship (with whomever) today? Do they stir your soul and create joy or a warm sense of coming home? Or have the words *I love you* become rote verbiage, spoken primarily because it's routine? I love you speaks small whispers to the soul sometimes, but what gets us to the mountaintops of high feeling are the actions performed that need no words to be heard, for they transcend spoken language, and spirit is moving in action rather than through radio frequency waves.

When has joy radiated from your core being just because you did something out of the realm of the mundane that spoke to the song of someone's heart? That is the great reciprocity of love, acting from heart and receiving, gratefully and fully, the gifts from Spirit.

• • •

My beliefs in God have been put through the test of hellfire and brimstone. When, as a child, I would see heavenly beings fly over the altar of the church, it was such a peaceful place for me to just sit in wonder. And there was predictability and comfort in the Mass. Stand, sit, stand, sit, kneel, and following the liturgy that was repeated verbatim weekly, with the words drilled into young and old hearts, alike. *Jesus died for our sins. Repent.* And so on. But, as I grew older, I developed my own, divergent view of sin, and in time, I found a non-denominational church where sin was labeled as Self-Inflicted Neurosis. I liked that.

In my freshman year of high school, I had a wonderful science teacher, Sister Mary Magdalene. She was a gentle soul with eyes full of crystal blue love and tenderness. She had an air about her. She glowed with love of her students and of God. I became quite fond of her and was saddened at the end of my first year in high school to learn that she was leaving. She had decided to move to a new location in South Bend, Indiana, where she would live a cloistered life for a while and help others on their quest for God's truth.

We kept in touch through mail correspondence throughout my years in high school, sharing updates on the basic goings-on in my life. She always wrote me lovely letters back, and my wish to go and visit her grew, as did my quest for direction in young adult life. I had considerable interest in joining the Sisterhood (and I don't mean *Sisterhood of the Traveling Pants*, either), so it had become high time to discuss this in person with Sister Mary Magdalene.

I don't clearly remember who went to Notre Dame, Indiana on that trip. Skotek drove for certain, and I think my two friends, Cindy and Renee, came along. I definitely recall, though, that we stayed on campus, and I found my first time at a college an exciting experience for certain.

The priest had a close friend named Digger Phelps, who was basketball coach at Notre Dame at the time, and I remember that once we got checked in to our rooms, we went to the court where basketball practices were held. There, Digger and the team greeted us with open arms; we all said a prayer before practice, and Digger gave each of us a small religious medal to keep.

I vaguely remember going to dinner that night. We did catch a basketball game, and I remember everyone chanting, "Magic, Magic!" As one would guess from my dearth of exposure to school sports, I was not familiar with any basketball terms or stars of the day, so Skotek had to explain to me what the crowd was chanting. It turns out they were energetically rooting for the renowned star Magic Johnson. I don't know if he was visiting the Notre Dame game as a special guest or what, but Magic Johnson was by that time a powerhouse professional player for the Los Angeles Lakers.

As planned, the trip included my visit with Sister Mary Magdalene, who lived not far from Notre Dame. Hers was a modest home, with little shed-like buildings in the back yard that Sister explained were there for hermitage. I asked her many questions related to her calling, and based on our conversation, I continued to have a desire to become a nun.

To further assess my interest in becoming a nun, I soon thereafter attended a daylong "calling" event in New Jersey. The event building was old and simple, as was the view, and after some serious soul searching that day and in the days that followed, I concluded it would not be the life for me. I resolved, instead, to attend college and study something involving special needs people. I think this was for a multitude of reasons, beginning with the fact that my sister with Down Syndrome passed at only six months of age when I was 5 years old. Also, throughout high school, I'd taught CCD to special needs children at St. Hedwig's every Monday night during the school year. In the beginning, the five of us drove up each Monday: Skotek, Anne, Cindy, Renee, and me. However, Skotek faded away at some point, so thereafter, I would drive up from Freeland every week. We also taught CCD at the White Haven Center to adult residents a few times a month.

Back to religion… I was such a strong Catholic during my teenage years. I loved to sing in the choir. It was a passion…singing. I felt my spirit soar when I sang. I was involved in all youth activities. I was even a strong Catholic throughout most of my college years. I do think, in retrospect, that somehow my faith got me through some very difficult times. I don't know when I lost it, but I did. I got married the first time in a little Catholic church on Nantucket Island. We had to use connections with the bishop to have it occur, but it did occur there, only to later be annulled by the Catholic Church at no charge.

Both of my daughters were christened in the Catholic Church, and when they were little, I would take them to church. When their father and I got divorced, I stopped going. I then tried Unity, which I did enjoy, but the children didn't participate actively in the services. Unity gave me strength in hard times, though, and for that I am thankful. I also met there the man who would become my third husband and in time the two of us were married at the Unity church in a beautiful ceremony presided over by a friend of mine. Later, our son Quinn was blessed in our living room by that same friend who had performed our wedding ceremony, but Quinn now goes to church only occasionally with his grandparents. We have church-hopped a lot to find one that fits all of us, but so far with no luck.

However, I did become an ordained minister through the Church of Melchizedek several years ago and have performed two wedding ceremonies and co-officiated at another. Do I practice a religion? I don't feel that I do. I do feel this was a large part of my life that is missing. I am not sure how to get it back or if I ever will, but I do sometimes miss it, and I often felt that I was somehow harming the kids by not raising them within some type of structured religion. Looking back in hindsight, it is not the dogma but the belief in love, kindness, and truth that matter. I have, through the years, tried to teach my children that one does not need a building to have God in his/ her life. I have tried to teach them that they can talk to God anytime. Well, I used to teach them. I have not taught Quinn much about God, and none of them think of me as being spiritual. They just think that my thoughts are weird.

I do not talk religion with many people. I try to keep the philosophy of harming none and the law of threefold. I am knowledgeable about the Bible and the life of Jesus as an Essene and Ascended Master. I am also knowledgeable about the basics of the Old Testament. My brother has turned into somewhat of a religious over-the-top kind of man. My sisters continue to go to church, I think. My other brother does not. Some of my nieces and nephews are raising their children Catholic; some are not.

Journal Entry of 07/17/2019

To have a friend, you need to be a friend, but I have historically had difficulty maintaining friendships in my adult life. I lost so many friends owing to my own seclusion and isolation over the years. Friends have come and gone in a kind of revolving door pattern, and this makes me wonder if it is necessary in my spiritual evolution process, or it is out of poor habits and patterns. Is it that I've learned a body of soul languages by moving from group to group, integrating what has been learned from each individual or group of individuals and continually moving forward, or, have I been in actuality moving backward without forming more durable bonds? I just know that I want to find my tribe and my divine soul life partner so that this vagrancy of shuffling around from person to person can finally come to an end. I know that life is an evolutionary process of comings and goings and constant change, but I would love some stability at long last. I had a measure of stability in a few relationships, but I don't know if I was ever very stable or present during those times. There always seemed to be some drama or situation going on that needed tending, some chaos or the other. Was I the only factor in these relationships? No, I certainly was not. Without delving into my second marriage for the sake of my girls, I will just say that my oldest came because she was destined to be here at this time, and my second child as well. Their father and I have much animosity toward each other, and he certainly did not make our lives easier when I married my third husband. In retrospect, things happened as they needed to, I suppose, but there certainly is not any love lost. They have each put me through a different kind of hell on Earth. I bless them and send love, because if not, hate would fill my soul, and I choose to rise above and choose neutrality. They are the fathers of my children, and I honor that role in my life.

My son's father and I loved each other even though we had many legal hurdles to jump over early in our relationship and intermittently as well. The human spirit can only take so much until it retreats and looks at situations from a different perspective. My third husband and I were married for many years, and it was my triggers that eventually wore me down, and my girls not being with me, that I think began our descent into a failed relationship and the marriage breaking up. It did not end well or peacefully. There is so much to speak of concerning these relationships that could be addressed, but this is not the time. Perhaps in the future it will have its place, but for now, it must be left as it is.

I hope one day to exchange full intimacy, but if so, it will certainly be taken slowly and with caution, for now intimacy to me is much more spiritually based than just the physical act of copulation. I know that it will take time. I allow myself this time to learn more about myself. I allow myself more time to integrate my soul parts back into myself so that I can be as whole as I am able. If I am to have a partner again, I want to make sure that I can give more than what I have ever given to any other partner. It will be a gift that I give to myself, and if I do not find a divine soul life partner, then I shall walk in solitude, enjoying this Earth ride.

Journal Entry

A glitch today, and something I cannot control. Paperwork, important paperwork, has not been submitted yet on my sexual abuse case, so I wrote some answers myself and sent them to the attorneys. I was so tense while writing, and afterwards, I spun. I spun and felt not in control of my mind, my body, my life. I wanted a drink, a big alcohol-laced drink. I wanted to dull my pains of times that I remembered today, and as I sit and write now, I assess how I could have handled it differently, without the tension and without the lack of control. Frankly, I yelled at myself and told myself to stop spinning, to calm myself. Sometimes things need to be stated out loud, even if it means talking to oneself. The premise of the writings that caused such stress in my body and mind were the things that I consider weaknesses in myself. Such things as failed suicide attempts, anxiety, and depression stemming from the abuse. They're the unspeakable pains that only a few hear about or even know about from me personally. So, as I write this book about my life, I don't look at it with rose-colored glasses. It's been a most difficult time in various ways, and yet I confidently tell you that you can also move through these dark times of your life. As I look back, I am not sure how I made it through some-times, but with God's grace, I certainly did.

I hereby acknowledge that I have a medical diagnosis of C-PTSD caused by the priest's abuse during my teenage years. There is no reason to hide behind the truth any longer. It's been a long, hard road at times, but I am alive. Here's the thing, though: I choose not to remain a victim. I choose not to remain in a state of grief. I choose not to harbor anger and hatred. I choose not to hold onto these feelings, because they are simply not good for me. Perhaps some may feel that I am choosing to hide it away and not address it, but I am a person who sees or feels that something is wrong with self and then looks for ways to heal or make it better. I am my own worst critic. Let me rephrase that, I have been my own worst critic. I am not living my life in a bubble, but I have been learning to set boundaries for myself and part of the boundaries is halting negative self-talk. The lessons that seem to be coming up these days are trust and self-worth. Trust in self, self-worth, and honest love for self, all these go hand-in-hand, I believe. I never thought that I could advance this far, and I am often humbled by what I have experienced and healed. I continue to strive to make a difference in this world. I continue to look for the silver lining, because sometimes looking for the silver lining is the best one can do at any given moment.

Journal Entry of 7/20/2019

As I sit and write today, I find it a huge responsibility that I have placed upon my shoulders to share my story and my journey toward healing. I accept that responsibility. I do not have all the answers, but herewith I provide you what I have done to heal over the past four decades.

Some say that a hero's journey takes place when one moves past the pains that he or she has endured through suffering such as sexual, emotional, and/or physical abuse. I think that we all walk a hero's journey, daily; some of us do not realize a hero lies within each person. It is my hope that this book will help you find your internal hero and your own inner compass.

We all face different obstacles that need to be overcome. Some face challenges head on and some prefer to bury the challenges in hopes that they will go away. Wherever you are on your journey, know that you are stronger than you have ever given yourself credit for. In today's culture, great atrocities to women and men are being uncovered and exposed, and there is a deep desire to release the loneliness that descends upon a soul whose plight is suffered in silence. We want the voiceless to gain a voice and help us determine what needs to be changed on our planet. This desire, I believe, leads to healing what has been broken inside. As I write the word *broken*, I pause to reflect that for far too many years, I considered myself broken. I was broken in mind. I was broken in body. I was broken in spirit. I likened myself to the bowl that has been mended using gold as used to be done in China, a beautiful way to embrace the experiences that have created cracks within the psyche. It is flawed in a way that enables the individual to accept the fact that he/she is broken and will only be repaired using materials of great value.

I realize that our thoughts and words have so much power. When I thought of myself as broken, a broken soul, a broken heart, a broken/fractured mind, a broken body, albeit true, I was also ingraining deeper in my psyche that I was broken. So, what happens to something that is broken? You throw it away. You see the flaws in it. You see the reasons that it broke in the first place if it is to be kept. I realized that every time that I felt or thought that I was broken, for whatever reason, a bit of me sloped downwards. Perhaps my shoulders slumped, my breath took a heavy sigh, a tear rolled down my face. This belief of being broken not only continued my inertia in being stuck in a pattern of lament, beating up of self, being a victim, but it also attracted undesirable aspects of like kind. I see this affecting my past relationships and my choice of men to become involved with.

Journal Entry of 8/3/2019

I have had a dull ache and pain in my lower quadrant of late and I wonder if it is related to cell memory trauma. It is my lower gut refusing to let the resentments out, I think. As I write this, I choke on my own saliva and I cough heavily, my way of knowing and releasing these days, and I do not like it.

Now, a reflection on the book that I just read, *The Disciple* by Simon Hay. There were many Aha! moments in it for me as I read the book and even after I finished it. There were passages for which I wish I had a highlighter, because I recognized things important for me to know and/or remember. Initially, when I began reading this book, I became very relaxed and sleepy, but not because its content was lacking, because of the energy it emitted to my soul. Strangely, it touched my soul in ways that I had not expected. I was told by Spirit that I would not be the same after I finished reading it, and I do, indeed, feel a shift somewhere down deep. Mr. Hay effectively presented Jesus outside the role of other-worldly God and introduced us to a real, living, breathing, feeling man. I must say, up front, that some of the sexual references triggered me. I can understand why individuals could be offended by some of the book's content, but in a realistic world, Jesus-God was man. He had the same human desires as any other man living and breathing today.

Now, a change of subject is in order, for I have thought of something seemingly out of the blue, although I realize that everything is connected to everything else. Here goes:

I'm thinking about being alone. I'm also contemplating why I resist learning my spiritual teams' names, and I realize it is because everyone leaves. That's right. Everyone leaves through growth one way or another, and I'm crying slightly, but I do take comfort in the relationship that Simon Hay has with Gegu. Simon is never alone because he has Gegu. I realize that I am never alone either as I have my "Ancient One" as I call him. Perhaps now I will allow his name to be heard by me and I will allow him to be my constant companion as I continue to walk this earth. I hate change when it comes to people coming and going in my life, but I have realized and I acknowledge that this is what is to be, at least for now. This memoir, though not epic by societal standards at all, has certainly provided me with many insights to myself, to the life of Jesus and his family, and to the path of becoming a more attuned healer. So to me, and I hope to the reader, it is personally epic.

Journal Entry of 8/6/2019

I have realized how strongly I dislike the timestamp of dates of events ever since Michelle passed, and yet some days continue to be etched in the psyche. The full date of the death of my beloved childhood friend, Michelle, is an unwelcome stamp in the memory, and I remember it not just with my mind, but with my body and my heart as well. It is because of this remembrance, that I now only choose to remember general season or times of year of those have who flowed out of my life like syrup running off a flat plate on a hot day. So, instead of remembering full dates of the deaths of my other loved ones, I remember seasons, months, moments in time. I remember events, smells, locations, and conversations of moments of great change from my lifetime, instead.

August 14 is coming soon, and it is a different type of time stamped date: the anniversary of that grand jury report release and the shocking, fateful changes that it hurled into my life. I have this date etched deep into my psyche, my soul. I feel it building daily, more and more, gaining momentum, and I can feel myself start to spin. My chest is becoming tighter. My body aches as I walk. The cough is more prevalent. There is a growing uncertainty about my capacity to overcome. In creeps fear, and I detest fear. It makes me feel poorer about myself, stoppable, weak, and weepy. I start wondering where I can go to stop this date and those feelings from happening, but realistically I know that wherever I go, there I am, and there is that date. There is the reality of what unfolded like a tragic shipwreck. I wonder who I can reach out to, who might understand or take my hand until I feel stable again.

Therefore, I write today about the pain that time stamped days can hold on a being. I will overcome and move past this coming date with valor. I will overcome the memories springing up from every axon and dendrite in my body, and I will rewrite the program that that day has attempted to stamp upon my being. As I sit, the words flow onto the page and I find clarity in the internal work that attends to my body, mind, and soul. I become centered and calm. I am establishing a game plan for myself that allows for the spiral of ascent, rather than descent. I have all of the tools that I need, right here, right now, to neutralize the angst, internal stress, and turmoil that was bubbling up. I have it all within me. I tell you this, not because I want pity, empathy, help, but because I want each of you to know that you have the power and capacity to move past tangles that linger around your being, holding you back from living the life that you have always envisioned for yourself. I promised myself that I would never lose my sparkle again, and with the approach of an anniversary of the event that rocked my world with hellfire and brimstone, I maintain a twinkle, sometimes hidden, but still there. I am healing myself and sharing about it here with you today in hopes that honesty about my process will provide you not only hope, but also strength that has been hidden deep in your core, strength to say, *Enough is enough and I deserve better than what I have been allowing myself.*

• • •

"I hate fucking triggers" was my social media post this morning, set in bright red background for the entire world to see. No, it's not like me to post such crude words onto a love-and-light kind of page, but perhaps today it was the necessary nudge-push that the Universe provided me.

So, were there one or more specific triggers today? Oh, yes! More Jerry Sandusky Pennsylvania State pedophile scandal again. It turns out that Joe Paterno knew about the accusations from the start and did nothing. So what were my emotions? Well, I examined them carefully, or at least I attempted to, and I found there extreme hurt, anger, especially repressed anger. It was not a pity-me kind of trigger, but rage that came from somewhere deep and dark in my consciousness.

So, I vented with words, throwing lots of "fucks" into the mix. Then, I attempted to regroup by thinking about how far I've come and the tools that have gotten me where I reside today, most of the time, that is. I chose to process my thoughts further by taking my car to a self-service wash, which worked great until I ran out of quarters before fully rinsing the vehicle. Ah, well, I proceeded from there and arrived at a group therapy session quite harried and anxious.

I requested a clearing from the group or whatever else needed to be done to help me get rid of what I was feeling, and I cried. I sobbed bitter tears, allowing myself to be a victim for a few brief moments with all the anger and frustration running through me. The group held space for me as I wept the deep-seated tears of an abused child that no one had helped. I coughed, choked, and expelled. Then I spoke: all that hard work on myself, all the skills I learned to become who I am today, how can they just flee after viewing a moment of news on television? In all of my logical and spiritual growth, why did I allow that moment to overtake me and then fail to call upon the skills that I tell everyone else to use? I told them I could feel the love they sent my way, and that a calm was moving over me.

And it's time now for me to find my center no matter what triggers come along. It's time to speak my truth even if a sense of fear tries to sneak up inside of me. The warrior woman I've become can take the teenage girl by the hand and reassure her. I will be okay. I am okay.

• • •

Sometimes you will hear things that shock you right out of your skin, make you uncertain how to respond or proceed. Sometimes it feels better to do nothing but doing nothing is something in and of itself. There will be a time for actively doing something, but with the initial impact, simply still your soul and connect with Source.

Do not let jolting situations take your God away from you. Maintain your faith in that higher power, your Divine higher power, not the higher power of mortals that walk the planet in search of souls they can challenge and shake their faith, but that source of which you are a bright spark.

I was taught about God in a highly structured setting of written dogma that was fashioned by whatever politics were deemed suitable at a given time (my strict Catholic upbringing, of course). I have also walked godless during deep, dark nights of my soul after my abuse finally ended. I have cried out in soulful pain and asked God, *Why?* I have studied religions and traditions on my own and found that what is more important than any set religion is a deep belief and knowing of a higher power. I believe in the higher power of prayer. I believe in the higher power of intentions. I believe that words contain higher power to heal.

I believe that love can conquer darkness and that meaningful forgiveness begins with oneself.

Closing Reflection and Update

In the wake of the grand jury report, I had to once more assess everything in my life. I look at things from a different point of view now, and it has been not only liberating but also enlightening for me. I know that I certainly am not the same person that I was at the time of the report's publication and, in the long run, this has proved to be a great blessing.

I have learned that boundaries are vital. Saying no is perfectly fine. Being alone is also perfectly fine. It is okay to be happy, to laugh, to have fun. It is more than okay, it's necessary. Joy has found its place inside my heart. I have been realizing my self-worth, my strength, my determination and what I want and deserve in life. I acknowledge that at times self-worth continues to elude me, but it not as elusive as it once was.

Regarding the dark years held secret so long, I know in my heart and soul that I am forgiven. My lost child forgives me, I am told inwardly. My God forgives me. Question is, though, have I forgiven myself? Yes. Yes, indeed I have forgiven myself and this is liberating. I claim my sovereign divinity of self.

Rising victoriously from the depths of deep soul trauma, my spirit answers, *Yes!* and proclaims in joy, *I am strong. I am wise. I am warrior.*

CHAPTER NINE:

Insights and Growth

Choosing peacefulness over anger — Please don't get me wrong and think that I lay claim to some elevated state of perfection; there are times nowadays when I become downright pissed at events that occur in society and religion regarding sexual abuse. And rightfully so. But one great difference now is that I assess my anger in the situation honestly and quickly determine whether it hinders me personally or negatively impacts my children, for I choose to no longer live in constant angst that serves poorly.

This doesn't mean I turn a blind eye to the atrocities going on in society; it means rather that I choose peace over anger. I look at history and see that hatred has caused mountains to crumble, seas to turn red, and skies to darken, so what might my anger, hatred, or sorrow create in this world for my children and their children? I am now choosing a road less traveled in hopes this road will become well worn and considered a superhighway in future. *Teach only love, for that is what you are* has been a mantra for me for decades. I believe it came from spirit to me many, many moons ago as a reminder as to why I chose to incarnate at this time on the planet.

If we are to evolve into a society that honors the journey, no matter what the journey, perhaps it is time that each of us looks inside for deep love and then emanates it to all mankind. The teachings of the Christ were love and forgiveness. When given the grace of God, what will each of us do with it? Will I lead the way by example, or will I fall away and live a meager life in my little cubicle of the world? It is from the challenge of spirit that we come into contact with our divine inner being and begin to see the smallest, dimmest of lights presented by each of us. It is in knowing that we are all of one God, the One, the Creator of All, and we need to recognize that each of us is perfectly imperfect.

Only in judgment of one another do we separate ourselves from our Source. Life gives us mirrors with which to see ourselves in others. What reflects to you currently? Are you seeing a loving reflection of your strengths, passions, and creativity, or are you choosing to see reflections of what you think needs to be changed? When we allow ourselves to see the Divine within us, it is then possible to see the Divine within all. To me, this is what loving myself means, to be happy with how I am in the present moment and who I am in the present moment, knowing that this is the only moment, now, that matters.

If I were to have read this page so many years ago, I would not have believed the very words I have written and would have blocked hope for a better tomorrow. As it is, though, I've made a conscious effort to avoid having the sexual abuse define my life, even though there are times when I falter yet and cannot see what goes on with me even half as well as others can readily observe. These insights of others can be of great comfort, for example when someone points out that you are a loving beautiful soul, just as they can be highly disturbing and eye-opening, such as the feedback that you are busy maintaining such a high wall that it forces out love, or the honest observation that you are destructively stubborn. Those last two traits I have reluctantly had to acknowledge in myself over the years, but heeding this valuable feedback allowed me to largely overcome them.

I also choose to let go of anger, hatred, attachments to outcomes, and grief as best I can. Those emotions, if left alone or left to fester, produce dis-ease. I mentioned earlier having had many of my body parts removed, but today I chose to heal the rest of my body so that I keep the remaining parts for the rest of my life. I had my uvula at the back of my throat removed to help alleviate snoring, and it helped for a while, but in effect, the actual problem was me not using my voice; my throat chakra was blocked and stifled. I had my uterus removed due to heavy buildup of endometrial tissue on the outside of the uterus related to the sexual abuse and traumas from my youth. Many years ago I was diagnosed as having pre-cancerous cells in my breast tissue, which overlays my heart chakra. I no longer choose to own these maladies, but instead I choose to transmute them by encapsulating them in healing light and love releasing to the Cosmos that which no longer serves me or my life mission.

Healings the Vatican could (and should) bring about — The Vatican has the power to stand beside the survivors of sexual abuse and make radical changes unprecedented in religious history. It would mean many clerics having to face consequences, and it would mean the church having to pay out money to those who had no voice in the legal system, but it would signal that the Vatican is serious about ending the madness that has occurred far too long. Yes! The Vatican and Pope Francis could join the cause for reform of the laws and work with legislatures in that reform.

They could also have each guilty priest or bishop admit publicly they have abused, and have them publicly apologize. They could hold other bishops accountable for moving pedophile priests from one location to another, thus helping to affect greater healing among survivors of abuse.

This would be in alignment with the true teachings of Jesus.

The Vatican could be a greater force for God by accepting responsibility for the lives of individuals and families that remain forever changed and by removing the titles of all those who were sexually, emotionally, spiritually abusive. By revoking all privileges, by cessation of their monthly stipend, by making them surrender to local law enforcement or to papal authority if statutes of limitation have been reached.

A bit more on the modalities I employ — Throughout my decades of therapy, I recall only one clinical person, Ginny, ever asking me to talk about my abuse, but that is fine by me, because my initial sessions at the Victims Resource Center were probably the only times that I needed to share this information with a counselor. My non-disclosure over the decades may have been my semi-conscious preference – therapy is client-driven for the most part – or perhaps my challenges and focus changed as I became older and took precedence over my initial trauma. In either case, though, some of the modalities that successfully addressed my core issues more so than my condition included Neuro-Linguistic Programming (NLP), Eye Movement Desensitization and Reprogramming (EMDR), shamanic healing, and Theta Healing that I have praised elsewhere in this memoir.

A major milestone for me was to accept that what happened in my life is merely what happened, not who I am. That is a grand outlook that I try as best I can to maintain consistently, but a weak point in me evidences itself whenever I sit in remembrance of traumas and revisit the pains and fears that got embedded in my past. That is, instead of always being the grown woman warrior, I sometimes revert to the pubescent girl. When this does take place, I sit with the emotions, feel them, and then reassure my younger self that everything works out fine, that she is loved, that she is safe as an adult, and that she is invited to come back with me into myself.

This process of re-integration of self requires tender and thoughtful self-care, in my opinion. In order for my younger self to assimilate, I honor what she loved in her time, whether that is a food, certain music, or a favorite pastime, and I thank her by embracing her with gratitude of her homecoming. It amounts to my own form of shamanic healing, a potent one that has been a boon to my healing, and one that works well for me currently.

If any of these modalities spark an interest in you, the reader, I suggest that you research a bit further to see if they continue to resonate with you, and then trust your higher self to guide you to what you need and where to go. Follow your internal compass. And if necessary, step beyond your familiar comfort zone in order to soar to new heights. Don't be afraid to fall; remember, instead, that angels fly.

Once I realized that the past is just a moment in time, I was able to release the what if's, could have's, should have's, and fully accept that life happens. What has happened to you, has happened, but how shall you proceed from there? I lived a large portion of my life with a backward-looking victim mentality, both knowingly and unknowingly.

So, at what point did I stop being a victim and take my life into my own hands? I did it when the children and I became abruptly homeless, when the man we lived with put us out on the street as I related earlier. It took that drastic event for me to say, *Enough is enough and I will never put my children through this again*! However, and this is vitally important, I also determined that I was not at all going to be bitter. I decided to dedicate myself to becoming a better version of myself. I needed to accept that I was seriously flawed in that I did not love myself and was repeatedly transferring how I wanted to be loved into someone else. I simply decided to learn what makes me tick. I went out of my comfort zones to find my passions. I continue to re-invent myself, for it is an ongoing process, and one is ever evolving. I accepted that I had been sexually exploited. I accepted that I had been diagnosed with mental illness in the form of C-PTSD. I accepted that my own family had dysfunction. I accepted all of it.

Bumps in the road are what make smooth sections so pleasant — *USA Today* ran an article about my life situation and, yet again, there was my personal truth presented for the world to view. The article included a brief statement from Skotek. This time, I did know the article was in process and that the defrocked priest had been interviewed, but I was not privy in advance to what he'd said. The writers had wanted my input for the article, too, but I was advised to decline at that time. The overall effect of the new article, though, has been to raise in my mind the place of hardship, heartbreak, disappointment and the like in our lives as ultimately positive catalysts, that it, as things that help us grow ourselves and be of greater service to others.

Without having experienced my vicissitudes, for example, I would not understand nearly so well what others are feeling. I might never comprehend the core issues that another person feels in a situation unless I've gone through something similar myself. So, how could I be a good healer, helper, or information giver? The Universe has brought it on pretty hard and heavy sometimes, but as everyone tells me, *You'll be all right, you always are. You'll land on your feet, you always do.* And although I may not manage this gracefully, I do always land on my feet, and for that I am thankful. Many times I go deep, sometimes too deep for my own good, and it becomes bumpy. But what's life without a few bumps? Without bumps and shadows, how can one appreciate smoothness and light? One needs both to live and learn, but balance is key. And this is what I'm working toward: balancing the yins and yangs of life and learning to laugh in fun along the way.

Tend to your own heart and healing — Too often, someone will bestow upon me their unsolicited and unwelcome advice on my love life, "Audrey, I hope you're not thinking about getting married again. Fuck that, you don't need a man in your life!" Well, so much for wisdom from people who think they know my life, people who look from the outside in and only see what they want to see and hear what they want to hear. While my choices might not have been the best in hindsight, those very choices have provided me with extremely valuable lessons about myself and about the human condition. And one important outcome is that I've never given up on love. My first husband, Pete, loved me with all of his heart. He saw my beauty and my brokenness alike, and he accepted all of me. However, not being ready yet to accept myself for who I was, I had much, much to heal, and had just begun that process, during which Pete was a shining light for me: valiant, honest, and caring. Yes, as has already been determined, that marriage ended, but it yielded many treasures. And from my other two marriages, I have three loving, beautiful, vibrant children.

So, while I have experienced plenty of heartbreak, I've also experienced profound love and joy. While I have lost much financially and tangibly, I've gained so much more inwardly. Therefore, anyone who fancies he or she knows me well enough to proffer advice on love and the affairs of my heart, please tend to your own heart and to its healing. I will never give up on love, because doing so would be like God giving up on me, and since I am a spark of

Divine love, I'm following my soul. I'm following my soul and will allow love to guide my life. Whether this means a union of some sort in the future, it's not any of your concern. It's between my soul, my God, and perhaps, my future beloved.

A powerful test of my healing — I was recently given a work assignment inside a Catholic elementary school! Obviously, I had grave concerns about being there, about returning to an environment so much like the one in which Skotek molested me. But I accepted the assignment, nonetheless, both because it involved a special needs student I'd had previously worked with and because I definitely needed the income.

As my first day on the job drew nearer, my mind conjured worst-case scenarios, but these turned out to be unrealistic fears of impending doom. At the appointed time, I ventured back into the familiar setting of Catholic school, with all its accompanying sounds and sights, including religious icons and doctrinal reminders on display everywhere.

Presently, I began to settle down when none of my dread fears manifested, and while seated among six wonderful teenagers, I realized calmly that I'd come full circle in my life. The reader may recall that I had taught CCD to mentally challenged young adults and mature adults while I was still a high school student myself. Well, there I was again with a challenged young adult student for whom I was to provide not only academic training but also spiritual training about Jesus and his mother, the Blessed Mother Mary, about the love of God for humanity and for each of us.

During my short time at that school, I stated prayers such as the Our Father and the Hail Mary, but I always avoided the Act of Contrition at the end of the day; that is, I respected the school's beliefs inasmuch as possible, even though I did not resonate with them any longer. I attended Mass a few times, finding that I could do so with some grace, until one day the young female cantor sang "Agnus Dei". I wept my way through the remaining service, tears rolling down my cheeks as my charge sat beside me. As a result, I started doubting that I could properly serve this child if I were unable to manage myself. As has often been the case, I was being unrealistically hard on myself, and in retrospect, the trigger in that Mass was actually a positive one in which my heart opened; those tears testified how much I had missed the beauty in that song and others, songs that once stirred my heart so deeply.

I managed well enough in the service to the child, but I did not process my challenges well, and I did not express what I experienced to my children appropriately. I fell into reliving the past too much, and the victim/wounded woman resurfaced too often to support forward motion in my healing. Crazy accidents began to take place, such as a bacon grease burn that affected most of one hand, trips and falls, and tooth/gum issues all during the short time that served at that school.

Simply put, I was not in the flow of my life, and I knew it. I had long talks with my sister about whether I should leave my job or stay, but we concluded jointly that I needed the experience in order to move past it properly; If I left abruptly, I would end up having to face the same issues some other way.

So I tended these duties faithfully for a short while longer and then moved on for good reasons. For one thing, I knew that this book would soon be published, and it would have felt incongruous to release my powerful story of what had happened at St. Casimir's Church and Bishop Hafey High School. Naturally, the reader and I understand that those two are not wholly dichotomous, but my experience has clearly been that first impressions and outward appearances often determine people's perceptions.

So, in time, I left the school and I am satisfied it was the right time.

I am grateful for my experience with the school staff and children in the bubble that is affectionately known as the Pickles Crew. They have a special place in my heart, for they welcomed me with warmth I did not realize I had needed. In that classroom I experienced such love, compassion, and respect, not only by the teacher and assistants but also by the children. They accepted one another with unconditional love and genuine concern for each person's mental, emotional, and spiritual well being. They reminded me that kindness, laughter, and music make a day filled with tasks go smoother and faster. They provided me with a greater understanding of what was missing in my life, where my heart needed to be healed and then opened wider. Those nine souls showed me that those who practice Catholicism with sincerity are intrinsically good by nature, and they helped me remove a spiritual barrier between the faith and me that I had not even acknowledged. In much gratitude, Pickles Crew, it was an honor working alongside you.

I Am — In keeping with the idea that I might have erected inappropriate barriers between my Catholic upbringing and my adult life, that I may have inadvertently "thrown the babe out with the bath water," I would like to share another startling revelation of this sort that came to me as I wrote out pages of this chapter. For even though it's totally understandable that I'd want to distance myself from memories of Skotek's hypocrisy and abuse — that just makes perfect sense — that fact should not necessarily negate what Skotek presented us in class. This startling realization has to do with concepts Skotek shared with us in that first catechism at St. Casimir's, a class I've discussed several times with searing condemnation, because the man was impersonating a man of God while carrying out devilish schemes.

However, the substance of Skotek's talk that day was not tainted like the man. The substance of his talk had to do with Yahweh. Yahweh, I Am. I Am Who Am. Yahweh, God.

Well, it has taken me forty years to realize that Yahweh, I Am points to one of my key life lessons. I Am. I Am divine. I Am a spark of divinity, and that divinity, I Am, is one with the Creator of all that is, the One, God, the Omnipotent. I Am one with God. I Am a part of the divine unity that flows across lifetimes and expanses of space and time, knowing no boundaries. I Am eternal love in constant flow.

Thus, all the events of my life contributed to the remembrance of my divinity and to the recognition of my free will to create as I choose. Those times when I was so frustrated, angry, and hostile toward God were indicative of what I felt toward self.

I Am thunderstruck. And to think this concept was presented by Skotek of all people. So much to consider!

Whether to tell my full story now, or to retreat into silence — When I awaken during the night troubled by memories, sweating and tired from tossing about, I find it helpful to sit up and write. Doing so depressurizes my psyche and keeps those troubled memories from venturing into my waking life. The magical thing about waking up and writing half asleep is increased likelihood your intuition can be heard more clearly in the drowsy quiet of the night when no one else stirs, except perhaps the dogs who raise their heads halfway to look, but then drop back asleep.

So, here we are tonight, and the perfect time to consider going more fully public with my story versus keeping mum, and that always begins and ends for me by weighing the anger and grief that accompany the question, and by reviewing the frustrations of trying to speak my truth the first time around.

Anger versus grief, which is it? Or both? Or neither? Have I repressed the anger in the name of being spiritual? Have I not faced the god of anger? And what of grief? Have I not faced the goddess of grief for far too long not to know her name intimately? For where there is anger, is there not grief at something that has been lost? Have I not yet walked in the shadows of both for long enough? Or have I just skimmed the surface of what they both feel like? Perhaps it's the target of the grief and anger that I have not yet welcomed into my space, but instead moved it inwards toward myself. The weapon of my anger, destruction, has not been visited upon the perpetrator and his ally, but rather upon my own soul, for maybe, just maybe, I allowed that connection with my God self to be harmed. So, was I the victim of my own self-loathing, of my own internal anger?

The answer is, *Yes.*

In pondering how I had allowed this to happen, I remember that I had not always owned the anger and rage that coursed through my veins. No. The fire moved me to find justice. The fire in me led me to find reconciliation with the part of me that wanted to look forward instead of back. The part of me that held fire was scorched and burnt by the hands of men of God who laid their hands on parishioners' souls to steer them heavenward, and yet who drove my own soul into a personal hell. When the fire rose and I took action by going to the bishop on my own, it was an act of taking back my power. It was a way for me to use my voice to free my soul. I had hopes that Skotek would be removed and would never play the role of priest ever again. And for a while, that seemed likely, but my hopes turned to rage at the men who would "do no harm." In those early years, when Skotek was placed back into a church, I had begged Bishop Timlin not to do so. It was a time before online maps and GPS, so I'd searched in vain for the church, because I'd been given the correct street address but the wrong town name. Then one day thereafter, I realized the error, and noted that the correct town was nearby, close to my work. Traveling there, I saw that the church included a school, whereupon rage, pain, and grief overtook me. I had repeatedly spoken my truth of Skotek, the man had admitted it, and yet he was placed directly into another church with a school. Although my account had been believed, it was very much as it had been overlooked and re-filed under, *Let's try again within the system.*

After all of those letters sent and calls made, Skotek was just given a new post, and knowing that the man who had raped my body and spirit was out and about, free to do it again, tormented me, so I'd reluctantly decided the District Attorney's office was the next stop.

I remember driving from Scranton to the district attorney's office in Wilkes-Barre, so nervous and scared, yet armed with ample information and proof in my hands. I was ready, yet again, for justice. I walked to the desk and declared, I *would like to report a crime,* and was escorted back to meet with two detectives. I told them how I had been abused by Skotek, how I'd reported it to Bishop Timlin, and how the bishop had then removed Skotek from our church and school only to place him in a different church and school. And I handed over my corroborating evidence in the form of hand signed cards, photographs, journals, etc.

Yes, I tendered plenty of proof, but I was not properly inter-viewed/questioned by the district attorney's detectives. Then, Skotek was allowed by them to grieve the loss of his brother with-out having been questioned, even though the female detective pointed out that the statute of limitations would soon run out on the allegations I'd made. So I told this female detective I wanted him prosecuted, pronto, yet she dragged her feet.

What was not allowing this to happen? Was it the district attorney? Was it the bishop? Was it both? Was it fear of tangling with the might of the Vatican? Perhaps I will never have the full answer on why my search for justice fell dead in its tracks and my anger turned to grief. Whatever the case, Skotek was never charged, and yet I stood trial figuratively for decades.

The untold story, now filling these pages leads me to ask if I should restoke the fire that stirred me all those years ago. Do I dare awaken the sleeping dragon of anger once again and allow her flaring nostrils to fill the air and burn away the remainder of charred debris inside my soul? Or shall I allow this rumbling, tossing dragon to find its place in sleep yet again? Already, I know the answer that will free and heal me more deeply at the core, but this warrior has not overcome all her fears of the flames, even though I have of late stiffened my resolve to do so. In coming days, I will indeed rouse the dragon and expose those unburned parts of me to its mighty flame. The pieces that had been left so long to smolder will again draw oxygen to their final burn and then eventuate to ashes, which will enrich Mother Earth and contribute to healing for the planet.

And so it is that the struggles placed in life provide the very pathways for renewal and growth. These pathways are rarely direct or smooth, and they are not meant to be. Without curves and bumps along the way, how would you fully appreciate steady going? Without rain, how could you fully appreciate the sun? Without darkness, the light can be perceived to grow dim, because ego wants more, more, and more.

I advocated for myself back in my youth when I was fierce and fearless. I used my voice to be heard to the high powers that ruled the local diocese, and then again used my voice at the district attorney's office. Something was eventually done, but certainly not enough, and the widespread lack of interest in seeking the truth has been worse for me than the abuse itself. Even some of my own blood family concluded I had an affair with the priest during my high school years. They say that I wasn't raped. But did they even come to me with questions upon which to base such hurtful assumptions about their own family member? No.

I was raped. I was sexually violated at the age of 13, and it continued for years. Society views rape as sex physically forced upon an unsuspecting target, but that's not how most rapes happen. Research it. Don't be blind to how prevalent grooming is… don't be blind to how predators condition the victim. Yes, I was a victim. These are hard words for me to consciously express, for I am now a survivor. I am a self-proclaimed warrior.

I don't hate anyone for judging me prematurely or inappropriately, and I forgive the ones who then distanced themselves from me, but I cannot deny the hurt this has caused me. It hurts me that not one has asked me how the abuse began. Not one has asked me why it continued. The account given in this book will be news to them, if they read it, and I hope they will in fact read it. I love them as blood family loves blood family.

Few people reached out in love to me as regards my abuse and recovery, but I am so very grateful to those who did.

Know now that I will not shrink my past into a corner to be buried again. I will not suffer in silence any longer, and I refuse to allow suppression to overcome my life. What I will do, instead, is to speak the truth straightforwardly, because there is someone out there who will love to hear they can survive abuse and live life with beauty and grace. I will speak the truth straightforwardly, because his or her life may depend it. I will speak the truth straightforwardly about how I lead my life toward healing and letting others know they can do the same. It is my soul path in standing in my truth and not sinking to something to which I am not. I claim my out of the box thinking and healing as a part of my process that will provide help and healing to those who need it. This is my hope.

CHAPTER TEN:

Letters, Poems, Inspirations, and Photos

A follow-up letter to Pope Francis when I had received no response in four years to an initial entreaty:

Pope Francis,

Four years ago, I wrote a letter to you about the sexual abuse that I endured at the hands, mouth, and penis of Thomas D. Skotek, one of the Roman Catholic priests under scrutiny in the Pennsylvania grand jury report. I was the one that the church paid the abortion for. I reached out to you in sincere hope to be of some help in this soul-breaking epidemic that continues to exist. I also asked permission from you, as Pope, to release me from the secrecy-binding document that I signed when I was way too young and under total mental duress. It was not known to me then that after the bishops met in 2002 in Texas, I was free to speak my truth. You made no response to me then to free me from my deadening internal silence that I had to endure, nor did you allow me to offer information as to how five years of sexual abuse, grooming, and conditioning affected my entire future. I wasn't asked how I survived and became so strong spiritually or what I've lost personally throughout my life because of it. You made no response to me then and I doubt that you will now. I use my voice now, once again, to reach out to you in hopes that true change can occur throughout the church. There are always miracles, and there is always hope.

As an aside, I no longer am Catholic. I no longer see Jesus Christ as a savior, but rather an ascended master. For this, I am grateful, for it is my strong belief that if Jesus walked this earth today, it would be the Catholic Church (temples) that Jesus would be walking into and casting out people (priests, bishops, cardinals) from pure disgust and outrage at the continuation of sexual abuse that is causing splintering of souls rather than soul healing.

Reach out to me as to how I may help. Allow me to help heal what your men have so callously broken… souls. Allow me to be a voice for those who can't use their own because of this blackness that is within the walls of the modern church. I need not your allowance, as I have the Creator's grace to guide me. It is simply a request out of the blessed seat that you sit upon. My light will shine brightly no matter. I will continue to heal and help others heal from the trauma their souls endured at the hands of your men.

With regards,

Audrey Yagalla

CC: This will go into my ACTS box.

• • •

I composed this letter to apologize to a specific girl that I learned Father Skotek had abused after me, and also to any and all others whose stories of abuse I'll never hear:

Hello Mary Claire, Mary Grace, or whatever your name may be,

This is to you and to all the girls who are now women that I couldn't help in time. This is to you and any other girls who came after me while I was healing and tending to my life. I am sorry that I couldn't stop (Skotek). I am sorry that my going to (Bishop Timlin) didn't stop (Skotek). I am sorry that the bishop felt (Skotek) needed an apology and outreach, but not me…and not you. I am sorry that the Bishop put him back into the church and school where you were, even after my protests and calls. I am sorry that the district attorney's office had detectives who went to his church. I wish that I had asked for non-biased detectives, especially the female one who felt that he needed time to grieve the loss of his brother while I mourned the loss of my teenage years. I am sorry that my voice wasn't loud enough back then. I am sorry that my voice wasn't strong enough back then.

I want you to know that I did try. I made every attempt that I could to have him removed, but the higher powers-that-be wouldn't have it. I wish that I would have contacted someone else, but I went through all the correct channels back then, or so I thought. I am sorry that I couldn't save you from those hands reaching for you and your innocence. I am so, so sorry to you and to your family, because I know what it feels like to carry these harsh realities with you through life.

I am so sorry that the system failed you. I am angry that the system failed all of us. I think I know your name, Mary, the girl from the church after Hazleton, but I am not sure. It was said in passing one day by someone that I knew. Moments get etched into memory sometimes; I remember the day that someone I had talked to was going to your school. Fright, grief, anguish flooded over me. I knew that (Skotek) had done it again to another young girl. I am so sorry. I tried. I tried with my heart and soul to have him removed, but the bishop wouldn't have it. While I blame the priest, I blame the bishop for not responding as a human being looking out for the children of the church. I blame him for the continuing abuse; I blame him for mental abuse and mental pain that he inflicted upon me…and upon you, by keeping the man who used young girls as money counters in a place of power, where he should have had none.

• • •

An affidavit I submitted in support of my second husband to aid him in seeking an annulment:

To whom it concerns:

Jim T and I were friends throughout high school. While he knew my past and the abuse that I had endured, although not to the full extent, I thought that I would be all right. I was incorrect. I do not deny this man an annulment. He deserves someone in his life that makes him happy.

• • •

Free verse I wrote as part of a healing exercise in response to a particular question about my trauma and my journey back to wholeness:

Invisible, I wanted to be invisible

My holy body
I haven't been kind to my body
And it has shown through via
My many missing parts and illnesses
I thought that my body was not clean
Just as I felt that my spirit was not clean

As I unify my soul
And bring all its pieces back together again
Because unlike Humpty Dumpty
I can
I am beginning to fix my temple
That my soul resides in

My holy body feels the ache in my heart and in my chest
As I release and release
And set free the burdens that it has carried for way too long
And in that release I cough, I choke
I almost drown in the turmoil that is releasing
And then it aches

Sometimes for moments, sometimes for days
I assimilate the newness of the absence
of the thick, gooey swampy mess
That no longer rests in my holy body
I nurture the ache
Knowing that it is a healing ache that needs tending to
With quiet rest and solitude

My holy body now welcomes
The warm embraces of another
The gentle touches of body-to-body and soul-to-soul
My holy body and my holy soul
Have purpose now
And I no longer choose to be invisible

Through the years of mending
A slow shift has occurred toward finding beauty
When I see my reflection looking back

• • •

Herewith, a letter I wrote to Pennsylvania senators when they were considering (and balking at) a piece of legislation that would have very positively impacted victims of abuse:

To the senators who are on the fence, or who are just saying no to Pennsylvania Senate Bill 261,

Thank you. Thank you for helping me raise my voice and open my heart to the injustices that you, as lawmakers, continue to perpetrate within our society.

How can this be a thank you for your stalled vote? How can I be thankful for your outright indignation to saying yes? Because it reminds me that God has provided us all with free will, free will to choose for self or free will to be the voice of others who have an inaudible whisper of voice, who need to flow toward the movement of healing. Thank you for helping me align myself more with who God has intended me to be.

Senators, thank you for bringing to light that the energy of money continues to drive free will rather than compassion for the human spirit and human worth. Thank you for helping me to realize that because you are actively choosing not to use your voice nor your power for victims and for survivors you have led me to find my voice. My voice will speak for them, until they are ready. We will join together in the movement of healing, with or without your vote.

Senators, it's time to create the wave of change. You have that capability. You have the power for survivors of Pennsylvania's voices to be heard. You have the power to begin the wave of change within our society across cultures and religions. I believe in my heart of hearts that if you are not for the passing of SB 261, that there is still time for your hearts to open up and see with the eyes of your soul. That is my hope and that is my intent.

Blessings to you.

Audrey Yagalla, a case from the grand jury report

• • •

A heartfelt letter to my estranged brother after I realized how bravely he had tried to protect me as a teen and how he had paid dearly for that attempt to protect me:

October 21, 2013

Dear Brother,

Please read this with an open mind and an open heart. I want to say thank you and I am sorry to you. Thank you for sticking up for me with Pop all those many, many years ago. I didn't realize what you gave up and the ramifications of you sticking your neck out to protect me when I was in my teen years. I only found out months after Pop passed why you stayed away all of those years. I honestly had no idea. I had an inclination that it was related to the priest but I did not remember or realize that you gave up seeing Mommy all those years because of trying to protect me. I am truly, truly sorry. I thought that it was difficult for you to see me because I reminded you of what happened to me. I thought it was your way of handling things since everyone handles life differently. All of those years that Mommy could have had with you and your girls, all because of Pop, the priest and you sticking up for me and what you believe in. Mommy loved you so, so much. She cherished you. In looking back, I never realized nor understood what it may have meant that day that Gloria, Quinn, Pop, and I came down to your house. I do now. I commend you on your honor and will to stand your ground.

I can't turn back time, but please, please forgive me for my stupidity, being so naive, and not talking to you all of those lost years. Please, please know that I have never meant any ill feelings toward you nor your family. They are in my heart, always. You are my brother, and I love you no matter what you may feel or think of me.

Your grateful sister, Audrey

• • •

The song "Prayer" as recorded by Kesha, speaks so much to my healing journey. Please give it a listen. https://youtu.be/v-Dur3uXXCQ

• • •

This came to me in a meditation and is a message from Skotek's late brother (and fellow priest) asking forgiveness for Skotek:

You've seen the pain
The Hatred
The Fear
You've seen the man in fright and weakness

Now the man is dying
And he is asking for forgiveness
He calls to you
His brother asks you to listen to him

Let him release his pain

Let him release his soul

So that he may find peace

In his passing

• • •

Portions of an open letter to family, friends, and supporters of my abuser, Thomas D. Skotek, one that recognizes the pain felt by everyone involved, and one that calls for sensible, equitable handling of pedophilia by both church and state to put an end to the silent suffering of victims around the world:

And this is to those men and women who think they know the truth about what happened because you know him personally. Did he tell you how in his words, "our relationship" began? Did he tell you about how he came to St. Casimir's Church to help save the parish? Did he tell you that the building was beautiful and needed work? Did he tell you that he started bringing people back? Did he tell you that he started youth groups? Did he tell you that people loved him? Did he tell you how old we all were when we were asked, only girls, to be volunteer money counters? Did he tell you how he talked to each girl's parents to ask their permission? Did he tell you that he learned some things during those talks that would help guide him in making his choice? Did he tell you that it was at that first meeting with all of us that he started deciding who he would pick? Probably not. Did he tell you that the money counting room was directly across from his bedroom?

What was his reasoning, if you were in contact with him then, about getting the security system put in?

But I digress. This man who is your family member. This man that is your friend…did he tell you of the first time when I was 13 that he held my hand in the car on the way home, playing a love song and telling me this is how he felt? No? Did he speak to you of the next time that I saw him, and I told him that holding my hand was wrong, but then he kissed me instead? No? Hmm.

Let me ask you this: did he tell you about the first time he ever touched my vagina? Well, let *me* tell you about this, his first time to sexually violate my body. He sat me on the corner of the bed and knelt eye level to me. I remember that I was on the corner of the bed sitting. I remember him looking for my reaction. Fear. I remember him touching me through my panties and watching my face. Fear. Scared. I remember him reaching behind my undies and his hand touching my skin and then my vagina. Are you okay? No. I don't like it. You will, he replied.

I remember the uncertainty of what was going on. I remember him touching my vagina when I was a young teenage girl. It's a movie reel that played over and over in my head for almost forty years. Did he tell you about that first time with me, when he took my true innocence away? No? Maybe you should ask him about that and all the other times that he had sex with me. Maybe you should ask him about how he taught me how he liked his penis held. Maybe you should ask him about how he taught me to put his penis in my mouth… because you know, if you put your teeth on it too hard, it would hurt him.

Maybe you should think and talk to him about all of these things… and then think of your sister, your daughter at the age of thirteen and her living through this. Perhaps you need to think about how you would feel knowing that a man thirty years older mounted a young girl and never stopped until she left and went to college. Perhaps you should ask him about the others in between and after me. Perhaps you should ask him about all of the ones before me, because I wasn't his first nor was I his last.

My family grieves through the process. I acknowledge the pain that your family feels as well, but I ask you to please, please see this for what it was and is, pedophilia. I understand the anger. My family is angry as well. I understand the confusion and trying to piece it together. We are feeling this as well. I understand the shame that all of our families feel. What I do not understand is how you can justify a supposed man of God claiming that it was all right to molest a thirteen-year-old girl. That is never, ever all right nor okay.

I am more than just the girl who had the abortion that the church paid for. I am the girl who went to therapy at the Victim's Resource Center by herself. I am the girl who went to the bishop by herself. I am the girl who implored the bishop not to put him (Skotek) back into the church with a school. I am the girl who told the bishop not to put him back anywhere. I am the girl who wasn't listened to by the bishop. I am the girl who went to the district attorney. I am the girl who took proof. I'm the girl who did this all by herself. I am the girl would not let it rest just because his (Skotek's) brother died. I am the girl who faced my abuser head on… and nothing came of it. I am the girl who, because nothing came of it with a district attorney, went back to the bishop on her own to see what else could be done. I am the girl who thought of a number, was told to get an attorney, and in turn was told that the number was too much… because the diocese didn't have that kind of money. The number was $90,000.

I'm the girl who followed and knew where he was and in what church. I am the girl who heard one day about another girl and her Mom having difficulties at that church. I am the girl who wrote a letter asking him to be moved, because I didn't think he was going to do it to anybody else (even though I didn't believe it). I am the girl who finally was able to get him moved by saying I didn't think he was going to do this to anyone else, all for the sake of helping another girl and not out of believing it. I tried through the years to have him taken out. (Bishop) Timlin never listened. He even told me one time that I said that it was okay to have him (Skotek) in a church again. I never ever said that. I am the girl who faced her abuser with a "Hi, Tom" while at a church bazaar… twice.

I am the girl that wrote Pope Francis in hopes that somehow I could help stop the pedophile epidemic within the church. I am the girl who was never given a response by the Vatican. I am the girl that married three times and was in relationships. I am the girl who was hospitalized, has triggers, PTSD. I am the girl that has held a full time job within a school system for twenty-seven years. I am the girl who never let her girls be cheerleaders because of the stupid cheerleading uniform she put on and was not ever a cheerleader. I was the overprotective parent who was fearful because of deep-set fears from her own childhood. I am the girl who doesn't manage money well even though I learned to keep a ledger in high school and even though I paid the church's bills and kept track of it all. I am the girl who hates cleaning house though I cleaned the rectory. I am the girl who hates shopping. I am the girl who gets frustrated in the weaknesses in herself… and can see the light in others, but sometimes not in herself. I am more than a survivor. And it's time for me to speak my truth so that mine, amongst many, will be heard finally.

I write this out of my love for humanity. I write this because I know that the Diocese of Scranton has attorneys and therapists that review cases even now. I know that they see the atrocities that come upon children. I can imagine that they, too, often wonder why the pedophile priest is not removed, but have no say in the papal doctrines that they are paid to follow. I know that this cycle will not stop until the institutions are made accountable to society's laws. One can contemplate society's lack of moral code. I believe that it is from lack of moral codes and ethics within religion that are creating the wave of allowance. Society sees it within the lawmakers, although not all, of our country as well. It permeates society. I believe it is the hundredth monkey theory in action.

Religion . . .
foundation
of our faith

Rev. Thomas Skotek

Sr. Regina Chassar S.S.J.

Rev. Connell McHugh

Rev. Maurice Raymond

18

187

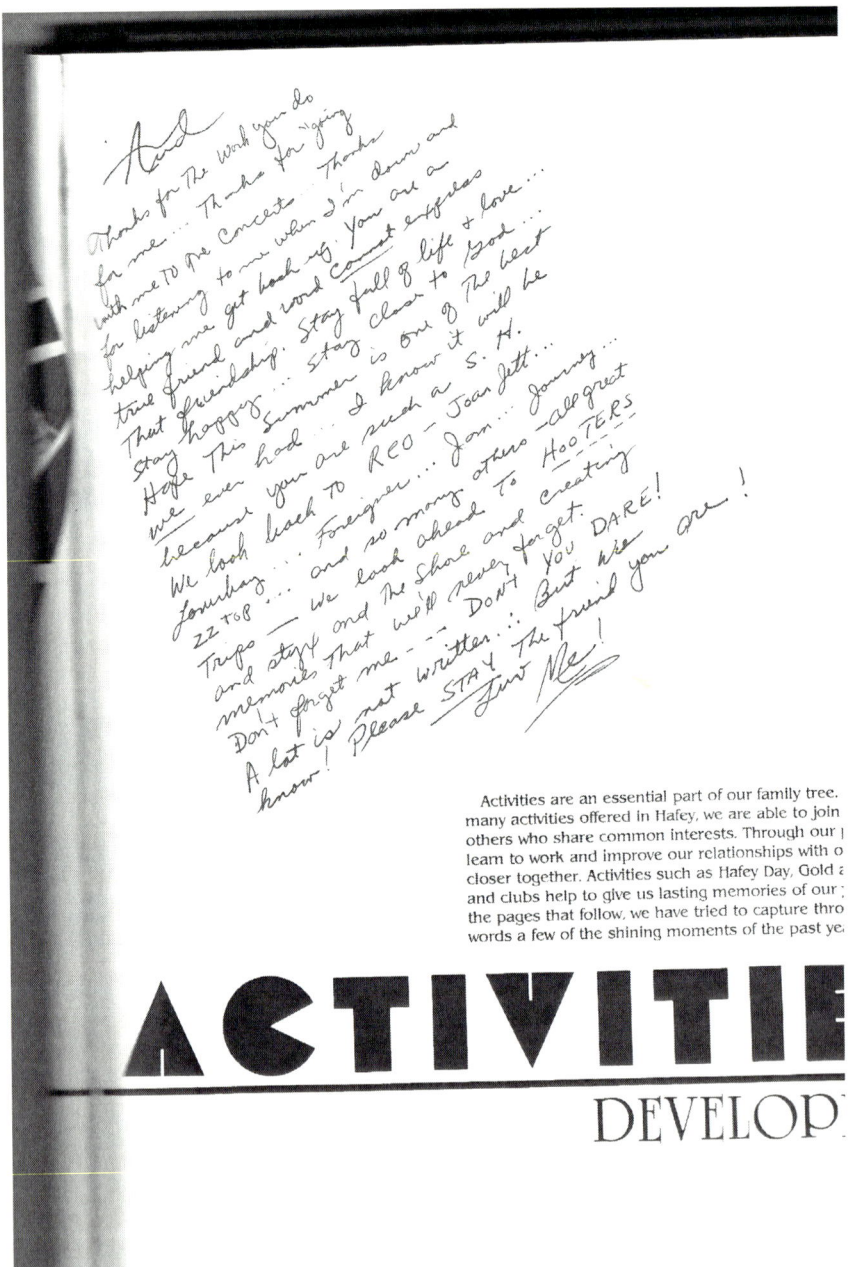

Activities are an essential part of our family tree.
many activities offered in Hafey, we are able to join
others who share common interests. Through our
learn to work and improve our relationships with o
closer together. Activities such as Hafey Day, Gold a
and clubs help to give us lasting memories of our
the pages that follow, we have tried to capture thro
words a few of the shining moments of the past ye

ACTIVITIE

DEVELOP

Hierarchy

Andrey—

One more step down the road
Will lead you were you want to be
and everything you left behind
Carries the mark thats you
all the love and life you shared
Will never be forgotten
A world is now much better
Since it has known you.

Now looking in the future
With hope and prayer and friends
You will succeed in all you do
The fabric of your life is true
Remember where you've been before
Remember where you're going
But remember where you are
right now – thats most important
Fr. Shu

Most Reverend John C. O'Connor, D.D.
Bishop of the Scranton Diocese

Most Reverend J. Carroll McCormick, D.D.
Former Bishop of the Scranton Diocese

Most Reverend James C. Timlin, D.D.
Auxiliary Bishop of the Scranton Diocese

4

190

Walk on a Rainbow Trail
Walk on a Trail of Song
and all Around You will be Beauty
Navajo Song

Florence Tanguch

Kim Poddo

Christine Messina

Terri Marchette

Nancy Yackim

Lexi Esposito

Erika Tongo

Diane Matz

**Congratulations
to the Class of '84**

Debra Liza

Cindy Silliman

**1983 · 84 Bishop Hafey
Teens' Cabinet**

Cammy Rivera

Lisa Garris

Florence Tranguch

Marsha Prevost

Ronni Notyo

Matt, Thanks for all the memories! I Love You, Michelle.	Pam, Remember all the great times we've shared in school and thanks for being my "Best Friend"! I Luv Ya, Michelle.	Congratulations Tina!! I Luv Ya, Ricky. P.S. I'm Forever yours Faithfully!!	Believe in yourself and your dreams, never, never quit!	Audrey, May you always remember what you've been taught at home. Don't be SAD, be HAPPY! Love God and we know you will accomplish whatever you set your mind to do, remember we are always here to help you if we can, and we love you always! Love Mom and Dad.	To: Mary Clair, Amy Alice Chico, Renee Kostic, Mary Kelly, Sharon Wilkenson, Sheri McDonald, Maureen Rossi, Pam Hommas, Pookie, Gina Magazza, Denis Buanato, Gina Usiclny, Lisa Schattie, Julie Dawly, Jennifer Oswald, Beth Mardynicek, Maria, Gene F., Carrie, Christy. And all the great girls we didn't have enough money to write about. We'd just like to say thanks!!!! Luv Larry K., and Leo K.
Pat	Gang, "Come sail away!" Love Meca.		You're listening, but you're not hearing!! Fr. R		
Duke says Thanks! from Perfect School Plans.		Diane, We love you, Love Mom and Dad, and Maryjo.		To: Maria, Renee, Pam, Jane, Diane, Karina, Lynn and Flo—Friends A shoulder to cry on, An ear to bend, Money to borrow, Clothes to lend, Friday night movies, Afternoon walks, Being together, Our private talks, Mending our hearts, Crying those tears, Planning our future, Voicing our fears, Our memories together, May they never end, Always together, Forever Friends Janine.	Q.S. I Love You!! What more can I say? / A.P. I'll cherish our rainbow forever I LY4 Ever! / M.S. Friends forever —Right? I love you?! / J.J. My #1-Boom ! Leo. Don't forget lunch, Randy or the baby. I A.H. Is nothing sacred? / L.M. W.A.Y.G.D? I Lylas 4 ever + ever / A.P. E.F. hutton / RARE I Love you all! R. and S Amy -Alice.
To my "7" best friends in the whole world. You were always there when I needed you. Always remember. May 7, July 39, Wildwood, "Moke," Saturday Sept. 1, "Blitz time," The Dogs, The four	idiots, Hey it's the girls from up in the mountains!!!, "Jazzy," Have a brewskie, New Year's Eve at Lynn's, And many more, Thanks for the best 4 Yrs.!!! Hey Bud, Lets Party! Luv Always BO-BO.	Hi Cindi, Sam, Sheila, Tracie, Sharon, and Lisa, From: Terri and Maureen.	Luck and love to the best of friends. Terri, Maureen, Sheila, Tracie, Sue, Cindi, Sam, Missy, Cheri, Damian, Mike, Theresa, Karen, Renee, Flo, Jane, Janine, Lisa, Lynn, Charlie, Diane, Maria, Karina, Shelly. Love Marg "84."	Pirate, 301, Tunes, Nectar, Blue Lights, Connie	
		TERRI + NEIL		Dina + Bob, Daneen + Franklin.	Sheila, Cindi, and "Crash," Remember, Labor Day '83, I'll Tumble "4" Ya!

157

191

Representative Tarah Toohil

116th Legislative District
Pennsylvania House of Representatives
Contact: Rep. Toohil's Office
717-260-6136
RepToohil.com / Facebook.com/RepToohil

<u>FOR IMMEDIATE RELEASE</u>
April 13, 2021

Toohil's Statute of Limitations Reform Bill Heads to Governor's Desk

HARRISBURG – Legislation sponsored by Rep. Tarah Toohil (R-Luzerne) that would ensure no agreement can prohibit victims of child sexual abuse from speaking with law enforcement today was sent to the governor to be signed into law after it passed on concurrence in the House of Representatives.

"My legislation makes it very clear that sexual abuse victims in Pennsylvania will now be able to provide information to criminal investigators regarding the heinous crimes allegedly committed against them, even if they signed a confidentiality agreement years earlier," said Toohil. "This long-overdue change in the law is a victory for victims."

To watch Toohil's video comments, visit

House Bill 1171 is derived from one of the recommendations of last year's 40th Statewide Investigating Grand Jury, which focused on clergy sex abuse in Pennsylvania. The grand jury found that Roman Catholic dioceses used confidentiality agreements to silence abuse victims from speaking publicly or cooperating with law enforcement.

Specifically, Toohil's measure would add a section of law which declares to be void and unenforceable any provision of a contract that prohibits the disclosure of the name of a person suspected of childhood sexual abuse, suppresses information relevant to an investigation of childhood sexual abuse or impairs the ability of a person to report a claim of childhood sexual abuse.

House Bill 1171 is one of several pieces of legislation approved in the House earlier this year by the Republican Caucus to provide better protections for Pennsylvania crime victims.

CHAPTER ELEVEN:

Final Thoughts

As this book is completed, I look upon my life in wonder as to how I survived it all. On a wing and a prayer with grace walking beside me, Spirit guiding me even in my darkest nights of shadow work, I kept a light, however dim, burning deep within the core of my being. Some saw this light as a bright beacon and others as a flickering wave in the winds of change, yet all saw it and it provided my soul with faith to continue the journey. And as I continue this path of soul in a human body, I have much to learn and share. I no longer see myself as broken; no one is broken. I am but a piece of Divine who chose this blueprint of a soul life to learn, to grow and to awaken change within the matrix systems that no longer serve humanity. We each are a piece of Divine. We are each a spark of Divine.

If the words upon these pages have incited anger and hate, let them not fester but release them to the ethers to be transmuted. We are here to encourage a new and higher understanding of who we are as light beings of soul. Each of us has the potential to shift paradigms within their own soul self and in doing so, create a whole new world, a new way of BEING. I have, through trials, tribulations and great awareness realized that love, forgiveness, and mastery of self are what is important. And this is my wish for each of you, that you love self, love others, forgive self, forgive others and master self so that you may be a guiding light to others in their times of shadow.